THE
WELSH
LANGUAGE
IN CARDIFF

Cyflwynedig i drigolion Caerdydd,
ddoe, heddiw ac yfory

Presented to the citizens of Cardiff,
past, present and future

THE WELSH LANGUAGE IN CARDIFF

A HISTORY OF SURVIVAL

OWEN JOHN THOMAS

First impression: 2020
Second impression: 2021

Cover design: Y Lolfa
Cover image: Llywelyn2000, Wikimedia Commons

ISBN: 978 1 78461 882 7

Published and printed in Wales
on paper from well-maintained forests by
Y Lolfa Cyf., Talybont, Ceredigion SY24 5HE
website www.ylolfa.com
e-mail ylolfa@ylolfa.com
tel 01970 832 304
fax 832 782

Foreword

RESIDENTS OF SUCCESSFUL modern cities seldom spend much time pondering how those cities came into being in the first place.

In the case of Cardiff, the amnesia seems particularly acute. Ask the average Cardiffian about the city's history and he or she will probably come up with something involving the Romans, a couple of Marquesses, a million pound cheque, mild ale and a meat pie.

It's a version of local history that has fetishized the small Irish community of Newtown, sentimentalised the multi-ethnic Tiger Bay and virtually ignored some of the most important people in the story of Cardiff, the Welsh themselves.

This Brains dark and Clark's Pies version of history is probably harmless in the 21st century but in the mid 20th century, when both the author and myself were growing up in Cardiff, it was insidious.

It was part of an attempt to paint Cardiff as a British city, not English exactly, but certainly not Welsh.

To speak Welsh was to invite sarcasm or even a slap, and the insult 'Welshie' was spat out with the same venom as the epithets used to insult the Irish and black communities.

That attitude was largely based on the myth that 'Cardiff has always been an English-speaking town'. It's that myth that this book conclusively demolishes.

Using sources as varied as personal and field names, court records, diaries and legal documents, the author shows conclusively that while the Welsh and English languages waxed and waned in the small walled town of Cardiff, both were always present, and that Welsh dominated the rural parishes that make up most of the modern city.

Even as late as the early 20th century Welsh was the majority language in some of the communities that make up the modern city.

While the myth of Cardiff being an English-speaking town is the author's main target, along the way some of the other Cardiff myths are busted.

It was the labouring classes, not the mysterious Welsh-speaking *crachach*, who clung to the Welsh language when the middle classes turned their backs on it and, far from all being sober Nonconformists, there were Welsh-speaking drunkards and prostitutes living out their lives in the city's slums.

The author's study of slander cases, the only court records which record the language used by the offender, is both illuminating and hugely entertaining, revealing as it does that drunken altercations were as much a part of life in the small seaport as they are in the modern city!

The account and analysis of the collapse of the Welsh language in the late 19th century makes for sad reading from a modern perspective. The author is no doubt right that that collapse owed as much to a failure by Welsh speakers to transmit the language to their children as it did to English and Irish immigration.

It is shocking to learn, for instance, that all but one of the Cardiff chapels which held their services in Welsh used English as the medium of instruction in their Sunday schools.

Rightly, the book ends on a hopeful note. Presumably out of modesty, the author doesn't point out that the survival and growth of Welsh in the city is largely due to a small but indomitable group of campaigners, with Owen John Thomas himself in the vanguard.

If I have one quibble with this book, it is its title. The story of Welsh in Cardiff is one of revival as well as survival. For that, and for this book, we owe a debt to Owen John Thomas. Diolch, brawd.

Vaughan Roderick
BBC Wales' Welsh Affairs Editor

Preface

IT WAS MY intention to write this book in Welsh – a language I learnt in my late 20s and hold dear to my heart, but illness has meant that I have struggled to do so. Despite this frustration, I hope that people who are not fluent Welsh speakers will now have the opportunity of sharing the passion I have for the Welsh language in Cardiff, the Welshness of the city and the surrounding area and the history of Welsh identity. They are inextricably linked.

The map on the next page shows the area under consideration. When I mention the 'town', I mean the parishes of St John and St Mary. The 'surrounding parishes' are Caerau, Llandaff, Llanedeyrn, Llanishen, Lisvane, Michaelston-super-Ely, Roath, Radyr, Rumney, St Fagans, St Mellons and Whitchurch. The surrounding parishes include well-known areas such as Canton, Cyncoed, Grangetown, Leckwith and Splott. As a later addition to the city in 1996, when evidence is available, Pentyrch is also included.

Though it goes against my life's practice not to use Tredelerch instead of Rumney, Lecwydd instead of Leckwith, Eglwys Newydd instead of Whitchurch and so forth, I reluctantly chose to use the English names for ease of reference. A map in Appendix B shows the Welsh names for the areas.

This is not an academic work as I wished to try and appeal to a wide range of readers, especially to those living in Cardiff or have an association with the capital. This is the fruit of research that has been a labour of love over many decades and that led to my Master's degree in 1990 on the history of the

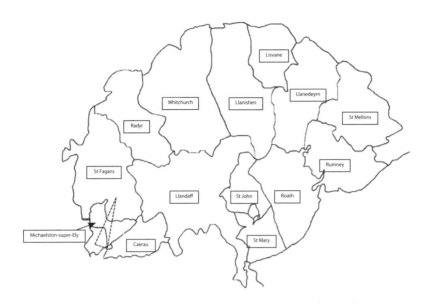

Welsh language in Cardiff. The bibliography at the end lists the sources I have used. I hoped to have undertaken further research, but illness has unfortunately made that undertaking impossible. In light of this contribution, I hope others will carry on the work.

I have included a brief history of Wales up to the Acts of Union[1] in chapter one. I have done so as it is impossible in my view to understand the current landscape without appreciating the past, and I'm well aware of the lamentable lack of Welsh history taught in our schools. This has led to many an ignorant view such as that expressed by Lord Neil Kinnock when he said that 'between the mid-16th century and the mid-18th century Wales had practically no history at all, and even before that it was a history of rural brigands who have been ennobled by being called princes.' It is vital to consider the Anglo-Norman conquest as it led to the initial Anglicisation of the town, Roath and Leckwith, and the history behind it shows how mistaken Lord Kinnock was in his observation. It reveals the stories of princes who united

Wales, others who bravely stood up against oppression and people who kept the Welsh identity alive.

In subsequent chapters I examine the names of residents and place-names in the town and the surrounding parishes and note an increase in the use of Welsh up until the 1840s. I also look at the lives of ordinary folk and their everyday use of the Welsh language, including during brawls in public houses which resulted in bilingual court cases with defendants and witnesses giving evidence in Welsh. I have cited examples of a bilingual Cardiff up until the 18th century. Other chapters consider the language of places of worship, with the vast majority being Welsh in 1845, and explore early education in the town and the change in attitude towards the Welsh language. Later chapters note the growth of Cardiff, its impact on the Welsh language which led to the re-Anglicisation of the town and Anglicisation of surrounding parishes. The final chapter looks at how the Welsh nation was rebuilt with Cardiff as its new capital, and the integral role the Welsh language played in that process.

Owen John Thomas
Caerdydd

Contents

Introduction

I AM OFTEN puzzled by the indifference some of my fellow Cardiffians and others feel towards our capital, who are only too ready to undermine the city's status. Without a capital city, the very foundations of the Welsh nation were frequently challenged. The Scots could boast of their capital for many centuries, so could the Irish. It was therefore with great delight for me that Cardiff was declared the capital of Wales in 1955. The announcement was greeted with enthusiasm by most of our citizens but unexpectedly not so by one of our MPs and future UK Prime Minister, James Callaghan, who said that his constituents would prefer to have seen extra cargo coming into the docks than Cardiff being made a capital. Yet he is honoured in many places in Cardiff, whilst others who worked tirelessly to transform Cardiff into a capital have been overlooked.

Callaghan, it would seem, failed to foresee the growth in stature that would ensue. By 1964, James Griffiths, a Labour politician and ardent supporter of Home Rule, had been appointed the first Secretary of State for Wales. When in office, he wrote:

Nearly a century has gone by since the nationalist movement *Cymru Fydd* had raised the banner of Home Rule. The fervour with which it had been acclaimed by the people of Wales gave promise of its early achievement.

Griffiths added later, 'But the years rolled on and still Home Rule became more and more elusive'. He died in 1975, leaving Callaghan to give carte blanche to Leo Abse and Neil

12

Kinnock to sabotage the 1979 Welsh devolution referendum. Their efforts were assisted by the incompetence of the Callaghan Government. The rejection of devolution in the 1979 referendum, with a 'yes vote' of 21,830 (13.1%) in South Glamorgan as opposed to the huge 'no vote' of 86.9% in the same constituency, was momentous. Cardiff voted against devolution once again in the 1997 referendum but by a far narrower margin. By 2011, following 12 years of devolution, the people of Cardiff voted 61.4% in favour of further powers for the National Assembly for Wales, located in the old docklands area.

Cardiff is often viewed as an 'English' town, regularly being placed in the same category as South Pembrokeshire and the Gower Peninsula. Even my fellow proud Welsh-speaking Cardiffian, the late Rhodri Morgan, believed this. As First Minister, he told a Canadian delegation in 2001 during their visit to the National Assembly that Cardiff had not been a Welsh-speaking town since the arrival of the Normans in 1100. However, this is a myth, albeit a popular one. Certainly, the incredible transformation of Cardiff during the 19th century with a hundred-fold increase in its population, turning it into a populous dynamic port of world renown, did have an impact on the language, but what was the position up to the 1850s? I hope that this account can go some way to demonstrate to my fellow Cardiffians and others that Cardiff has a long and close association with the Welsh language.

My own family's connections with Cardiff go back to the 1830s. My grandfather and his brothers worked in the docks in Cardiff. Unfortunately, my great-uncle drowned in the West Bute Dock in 1860, its basin now known as Roald Dahl Plass in front of the Wales Millennium Centre. I was born just a month after the beginning of the Second World War, above my father's pharmacy shop on Albany Road which he kept for nearly 60 years from 1927 until the late 1980s. My six children were born in Cardiff and my grandchildren were raised here.

All have contributed in different ways to the Welsh language in Cardiff. My wife, Siân, has spent most of her adult life introducing Welsh to children from English-speaking homes. She was the first head teacher of Ysgol Glan Morfa in Splott, the first local Welsh-medium school in Cardiff where most of the children walked to school – something the first pupils of Welsh-medium education in Cardiff could only dream of as they travelled many miles on a daily basis by bus to school.

Cardiff and the Welsh language have come a long way. It seems an age away now that in the 1970s supporters of the Welsh language in Cardiff were arguing for the right to keep Welsh street names such as Heol Llanishen Fach, challenging the absurd view that placing Welsh names on road signs was 'dangerous' and 'life threatening'. The Cardiff of 2020 is a bustling capital city with its own bilingual legislature and thousands of children being educated through the medium of Welsh. In 2019, Welsh-medium education celebrated 70 years of existence in Cardiff. From small acorns oak trees grow and to date there are now 17 primary schools and three secondary schools providing education through the medium of Welsh in Cardiff. However, to comprehend today we must understand our past and the history of the Welsh language in our capital city – an important story that is often ignored or even dismissed by our historians.

CHAPTER 1

History is the Conqueror's

HISTORY IS THE conqueror's version of events wherein the victor's role is inflated and embellished whilst that of the vanquished is either derided or ignored. The history of the Welsh language in Cardiff has often been ignored and to fully understand the situation we need to consider the history of the Welsh nation.

Cardiff, or Caerdydd in Welsh, comes from the original Caerdyf 'Caer ar Daf'. This translates to fort on Taff – the Taff is the main and central river out of three that runs through Cardiff. A roman fort was built in Cardiff in AD 75 on the banks of the Taff. Professor Hywel Wyn Owen believes that, as it was Caerdyf rather than Caerdaf, our capital's name is a very old name indeed and comes from the Brythonic language prior to the Welsh language which developed from its mother tongue.

When the Romans left Britain around 410, they left behind an island occupied largely by Romano-British Celts. Shortly after the departure of the Romans, waves of Anglo-Saxons swept across the east of Britain. Their advance appears to have been easy as the Celts who dwelt in the more Romanised region in the east of Britain were criticised by Gildas for yielding so easily to the barbarism of the pagan Angles and Saxons. On the mainland of Europe the Celts were widely dispersed, and thus easily assimilated within Latin civilisation. The Celts of the west of Britain alone retained their own language, which still survives 1,600 years later.

By the year 550, the Anglo-Saxons had established control of the east of Britain as far north as present-day Whitby in Yorkshire and as far west as present-day Bournemouth. The Romano-British peoples, especially those of Somerset, Wiltshire and Dorset, faced the onslaught of the Saxon invaders during those crucial times. Wansdyke in Somerset was built to resist the Saxon attacks from a northern direction. In the Battle of Dyrham in 577, three Romano-British forces were defeated and the towns of Bath, Cirencester and Gloucester were overwhelmed. With that setback, the whole of the land as far as the Severn estuary came under the control of the Saxons.

Thus the land that became Wales and both Gloucestershire and Herefordshire was cut off from the Welsh of Dorset, Somerset, Devon and Cornwall. In the following years, 600 to 650, the Saxons became supreme, spreading further west into Somerset and later into Dorset and Devon.

Similarly, in the north, the formation of the strong kingdom of Northumbria under Æthelfrith led to the Saxons thrusting westward and ultimately southward, culminating in the Battle of Chester in 615. The Saxon leader made his attack against the Cymry of north Wales, killing the ruler of Powys and also slaughtering the 1,200 monks of Bangor Iscoed (according to Beda). This battle effectively separated the Welsh of Wales from those of Cumbria and Strathclyde. In 633 Cadwallon, the King of Gwynedd, made an alliance with Penda of Mercia and their joint forces overthrew the Northumbrians and slew King Edwin at the Battle of Heathfield. Cadwallon occupied Northumbria briefly but lost his life at the Battle of Heavenfield in 634. With Welsh support, however, the Mercians were successful in their invasion of Northumbria in 655 but, with the death of Penda at Winwaed Field, they suffered a great setback. Commenting on the death of Cadwaladr, King of Gwynedd, from the plague in

681, centuries later the author of *Brut y Tywysogion* declares: 'And from then on, the Britons lost the crown of the kingdom and the Saxons won it.'

The building of Offa's Dyke by the Mercians around 784 marked out the frontier between the emerging nations of Wales and England. The Mercians however did not honour the frontier and invaded Gwynedd and Powys in 822, destroying the fortress of Deganwy.

With a succession of effective leaders however, Wales survived the invasions of both the Norsemen and the Saxons. Rhodri Mawr (*c.*820–878) united three of Wales' kingdoms: Gwynedd, Powys and Deheubarth, including Gower. He fought against the Danes with tremendous success, winning a huge victory in 856 when the Danish leader Horm was slain. Orme's Head at Llandudno was so-named to remind us of this triumphant victory of the Welsh over the Danes. The extent of Rhodri's victory can be seen when compared with the slaughter wrought by the Danes in Ireland, the north of England, large areas of Scotland, and in the major cities on the European mainland; namely, Paris, Orléans, Seville, Cádiz, Pisa, Hamburg and more.

Hywel Dda (*c.*890–950) was known as Hywel the Good, which is a unique compliment for a king. He was known also as 'the Prince of all Wales'. He united Gwynedd, Powys, Dyfed and Deheubarth and kept the Norsemen at bay. He minted coins entitled 'Houael Rex'. His recognition as a leader enabled him to co-ordinate the laws of Wales by calling representatives from all parts of the country to Whitland to discuss and agree the laws. The laws of Hywel Dda, as they became known, remained in place for over 600 years and even after the Acts of Union 1536–42 people still referred to the laws of Hywel Dda in settling matters. The laws succeeded in strengthening the sense of unity amongst the people of Wales. His laws and literature were the splendour of Wales. 'From an intellectual standpoint,' says Joseph Loth, the Celtic historian, 'the laws give the Welsh their greatest claim to fame.' Ferdinand Walter, a German jurist and professor at the University of Bonn, states in *Das alte Wales*: 'In Wales fairness and justice has blossomed, based on the laws of Hywel Dda in beautiful perfection that one would not have its equal amongst any other of the peoples in the Middle Ages.'

Owain, the son of Hywel Dda, ruled quietly over Dyfed and Deheubarth from 952 to 986, whilst England had been made a part of the Danish empire. Maredudd ab Owain, his son, came to the throne in 986, but the burden of government had rested upon him during the latter years of his father's reign. He had added Gwynedd to his domain some years before that. It was a difficult and disturbing time and Maredudd had to withstand attacks from the Saxons and challenges to his authority from within. The main troubles, however, were the Danish attacks that overthrew the Anglo-Saxons during Maredudd's reign. Even though the Danes failed to occupy Wales, their terrible attacks were destructive, especially on monasteries and churches. In the '80s and '90s of the 10th century, St Davids was plundered four times and the bishop was killed. On Anglesey, in 971, the Danes took 2,000 people as slaves. Throughout his reign, Maredudd was king of all Wales except for Glamorgan and Gwent.

Gruffudd ap Llywelyn, *c*.1007–1063, also known as Gruffudd of Gwynedd and Powys, led an army into Deheubarth in 1041 and also took control of Dyfed and Brycheiniog. Only Morgannwg and Gwent remained outside his control and the conquest of these two was soon brought within his domain in 1055. As a consequence, there was political unity in Wales for the first time. He did more than defeat the Saxons on the border. He extended the frontier in 1039, reclaiming lands previously taken by Mercia. The boundary of Gwynedd was pushed beyond Offa's Dyke by restoring the towns of Prestatyn, Holywell, Flint, Wrexham, Hawarden, Merton, Whitford, Hope and the whole of Maelor. In Powys, Welshpool, Edderton,

Forden, Thornbury, Hopton and many more were reclaimed, and along the eastern edge of Radnorshire: Knighton, Radnor, Waterdine, Kington, and Huntington. Most of these gains have remained inside Wales to this day. Gruffudd had taken 15 years to embrace the whole of Wales under his control. In 1056 he had to defend his kingdom once again against the Saxons when Leofgar, the militarian Bishop of Hereford, was appointed to take charge of the army and its soldiers as well as the Church and its priests. Soon Leofgar ventured to lead the hosts of Herefordshire to attack Wales. When Gruffudd met Leofgar's army in battle near Glasbury, the bishop-come-general was killed and his army was overwhelmed and destroyed.

Facing the Anglo-Normans

Within only a few years of the Norman Conquest of England in 1066, the conquerors had formed an understanding with the conquered and, as Anglo-Normans, they turned their attention to Wales, thus beginning a struggle with the Welsh that lasted intermittently for almost 350 years.

The initial invasion of Wales by the Anglo-Normans, c. 1086–1100, affected largely the border areas and coastal plains of the south-east where penetration involved least resistance. Radnor, Builth, Brecknockshire, Monmouth, Ewyas, Abergavenny and Caerleon fell to the invaders, and the low-lying areas of Morgannwg were also overwhelmed by Robert Fitzhamon, Baron of Gloucester, who built a motte-and-bailey castle within the ruins of the Roman fort at Cardiff. Slowly a small town was built around the castle and Cardiff was created a Borough in 1100. The hills and valleys of Morgannwg, however, were left in the control of the native rulers.

In north Wales, Hugh of Chester had built Norman castles along the northern coast at Bangor, Caernarfon and Aberlleiniog.

Rhys ap Tewdwr (1045–1093) ruled over Deheubarth (composed of Pembroke, Carmarthen and Ceredigion) and was killed in a battle near Brecon in 1093. The Earl of Shrewsbury largely conquered his domain, and Wales it seemed was close to coming under Anglo-Norman rule. However, in 1094, there was a powerful revolution throughout north Wales, which spread to the south. Anglo-Norman conquests west of the River Conwy were regained by the Welsh, together with Ceredigion and much of Dyfed in west Wales, leaving Pembroke in Anglo-Norman possession. Twice royal expeditions entered Wales with a view to restoring their recent gains but succeeded only by allowing the native lords in the south-east to regain their rights. Remote parts in the north and west also returned to Welsh hands, and for some time a balance was struck between the Welsh and the Anglo-Normans.

Anglo-Norman administration in the Cardiff area

The castle in Cardiff and in other towns was the focal point of the Anglo-Norman administration, housing the offices of the lord, the exchequer and chancery. The castle also served as a court for trials and as a gaol. It must be borne in mind that the Anglo-Normans were alien invaders amongst a hostile population and their courthouse needed to be guarded against attacks. Each lordship would have only one prime castle, with minor ones to serve lesser lordships. The lord held certain land in each lordship that he developed as a manor on a feudal model. The unfree tenants of the area would carry out agreed agricultural services such as ploughing, harrowing, harvesting, and make payment in money or in kind in return for their homestead in the village and for their share of the plots in the great open fields.

The trade of the lordship was confined to the borough for the burgesses who had a monopoly of trade therein. They paid to the lord a fixed sum annually in return for the right to collect the town dues and to elect their own officers. These privileges were enshrined in the town charter under which the town was governed; each town being a separate unit of government. The castle, the manor and the borough represented the foreign elements in the lordship and were located usually in the lowland parts which, as the area of foreign settlement, formed the 'Englishry' of the lordship, where knight and freeman held their land directly from the lord. The remainder of the lordship, the hilly parts known as the 'Welshry', continued to be held by the Welsh, living their own way of life in scattered homesteads and paying to the Norman lord the tribute they were accustomed, in the past, to paying the Welsh ruler. The earliest castles of the Norman period were simple wooden buildings consisting of a motte-and-bailey. Later on, in the face of improved methods of siegecraft used by the Welsh, the keep was built in stone. By the earlier part of the 13th century, it was necessary to construct powerful stone-built castles. Robert of Gloucester rebuilt Cardiff Castle in stone in the 12th century before the sixth Earl of Gloucester carried out further works in the second half of the 13th century.

Beyond the castle and the town, the Anglo-Norman community gradually cleared the fields of Roath and extended their base to Caerphilly Mountain. It is likely that those dwelling in the hamlets of Lisvane, Llanishen and Llanedeyrn were groups of unfree serfs, paying their ancient dues under the Welsh system but by now to their Norman lords for whom they would carry out some farming duties. It appeared to be a remarkable arrangement, where the conquered held their land and maintained their language. In the Minister's account of 1392, Penylan hill was described as Walshmenhull (Welshmen's Hill) which suggests that the Welsh had been living at the top of the hill towards Llanedeyrn and the Normans were in the lowlands of Roath.

West Wales and north Wales, c.1100–1197

In 1108 and 1109, Henry I, who reigned between 1100 and 1135, took control of Pembroke and then built the castle of Carmarthen. He then granted the lordship of Kidwelly to the

Bishop of Salisbury, and to the Earl of Warwick the lordship of Gower. Only Cantref Mawr, bounded by the rivers Tywi, Teifi and Gwili, remained in the hands of the Welsh ruler Gruffudd ap Tewdwr, whose father had held the whole of Deheubarth (consisting of Pembroke, Carmarthen and Ceredigion). On the death of Henry I in 1135, with civil war in England, the Welsh capitalised on the situation and repossessed Deheubarth. Likewise, in the north the Anglo-Normans were driven back to the outskirts of Chester. Though the Welsh had not taken full advantage of the situation, their uprising was on the scale of a national resurgence and influenced the independence of Gwynedd, Powys and Deheubarth for over a hundred years. Later, however, Henry II retook Carmarthen, the Norman families of the Cliffords regained Llandovery, and the Clares took Ceredigion. But before the year was out, they were displaced by Rhys ap Gruffudd who, by 1155, had brought all parts of Deheubarth under his sole rule. Between 1158 and 1163, four successive expeditions were led by the English king against Rhys. On each occasion Rhys was forced to submit and the Norman lords were restored to the lands, but no sooner had Henry II withdrawn that Rhys repudiated the terms and kept control of his domain. The period of the civil war in England had witnessed a growing spirit of cooperation on the part of the Welsh under the leadership of Owain Gwynedd and Rhys ap Gruffudd. Henry II, in dispute with the Church and the barons of his realm, could not impose his will and came to an agreement with Rhys by conceding Deheubarth, including Ceredigion and Llandovery. He also granted Rhys the title 'Lord of Ystrad Tywi', and appointed him as his intermediate in affairs concerning the independent Welsh rulers in south Wales and in their relations with the English Crown or with the Marcher Lords. Under Rhys' leadership, the Welsh had become skilled in the art of siege warfare and the use of siege engines, making them more than a match for the Anglo-Normans.

Ifor ap Meurig (Ifor Bach) and William, Earl of Gloucster, 1158

William, Earl of Gloucester, held the Lordship of Glamorgan from his main fortress at Cardiff. An understanding existed between successive Norman Lords and the native lords of Senghenydd[2], inasmuch as the upland areas of Senghenydd would comply with the traditional Welsh laws and rights. Whilst, on the other hand, the lowland section Cibwr would be ruled in accordance with Norman law. The earl took it upon himself to ignore the rights of Ifor ap Meurig, Lord of Senghenydd, who in response attacked Cardiff Castle at night-time by scaling the walls of the keep, taking William, Earl of Gloucester, and his family prisoners and holding them captive in the mountains until the earl agreed to restore the rights he had taken from the Welsh.

In 1183–84, the Glamorgan Welsh again attacked Anglo-Norman towns. This time, as well as Cardiff, Kenfig and Newport sustained great damage and expense to the towns and castles.

The death of Henry II in 1189 freed Rhys ap Gruffudd from his concordat with the Crown and he quickly attacked the Norman lordships of west Wales and brought all, but Pembroke, under his rule. Carmarthen was the focal point in the west, which had been held by the Crown since 1109 and, shortly after the death of Rhys in 1197, King John took possession of Cardigan, thus strengthening the English Crown's hold on Wales.

Wales in the 13th century

With the death of Rhys, the Deheubarth declined following dissension amongst his sons. Powys too was split into two parts: Powys Fadog in the north and Powys Wenwynwyn in the south. The Welsh resistance was now led by Gwynedd. After a long time of internal strife, Llywelyn, son of Iorwerth, son of Owain Gwynedd, also known as Llywelyn Fawr (the Great), seized power from his uncles and, by 1199, he ruled over the whole of Gwynedd. Under his leadership Gwynedd, and indeed Wales, began its greatest period when it reached a level of unity not previously achieved. Llywelyn's first steps were to reinforce his standing within Gwynedd by driving the Normans to the boundary of Chester and bringing Meirionnydd and Pen Llŷn under his control. His further plans were frustrated at first by King John who had the support of those Welsh leaders who feared the rise of Llywelyn's power. King John invaded Gwynedd and Llywelyn was forced to submit.

Problems in England, however, restrained the king from pursuing his victory in Gwynedd. The constitutional struggle in England led to the grant of Magna Carta and Llywelyn joined with the English barons, using the opportunity to attack Royalist lords in Wales. He gained the support of Welsh rulers, including the heirs of the Lord Rhys, and together they recovered considerable territories for the Welsh. In 1216, at a great council of Welsh rulers held in Aberdovey, he shared the conquered land amongst the rulers of Deheubarth and arbitrated on the claims in dispute. At the Council of Aberdovey he was acknowledged as the overlord and leader of all independent Wales. From this time the various leaders appear to hold their lands from him. From 1230 Llywelyn went under the title of Prince of Aberffraw and Lord of Snowdonia. The independent kingdoms of Wales were, therefore, linked together in the person of the prince who answered on their behalf in all external relations. In this way the king was no longer able to play one ruler against another, or otherwise profit as a result of their dissension. Having underpinned the unity of an independent Wales, Llywelyn endeavoured to secure its future by adopting the principle of single succession, in place of the customary practice of equal division of inheritance among all male heirs. During his lifetime his position remained unchallenged by the native rulers or by the Marcher Lords, against whom he conducted punitive campaigns in 1218, 1231 and 1233. He did much to win over the people, and share the belief that they were part of a single political and cultural inheritance.

After the death of Llywelyn Fawr in 1240, his son Dafydd failed to hold the territories bequeathed to him by his father, whilst King Henry III sowed discontent amongst Dafydd's brothers. His half-brother, Gruffydd, the first-born son of Llywelyn Fawr but not the chosen heir, was imprisoned in the Tower of London by Henry III and died whilst trying to escape from the tower by using sheets and cloths as a rope that broke under his weight. Dafydd also died suddenly in 1246, and an English royal army from Deheubarth advanced into Gwynedd and forced the surrender of the two young rulers, the nephews of Dafydd and the sons of Gruffydd: Llywelyn ap Gruffudd (ein Llyw Olaf – our last leader) and Owain ap Gruffudd. A new treaty, Woodstock 1247, forced the rulers of Gwynedd to hold their kingdom for the king and imposed punitive conditions upon them. The king took directly that part of Gwynedd lying to the east of the River Conwy.

Wales remained in subjection for eight years thereafter. In 1255, Llywelyn ein Llyw Olaf, grandson of Llywelyn Fawr, regained the lands west of the Conwy, with the exception of the castles of Dyserth and Deganwy. He then advanced into Deheubarth, taking Ceredigion, including the royal lands of Llanbadarn, and placed them in the hands of Maredudd ab Owain, the great-grandson of the Lord Rhys. Llywelyn then took Buellt, west of the River Wye, and moved into the Tywi Valley where Maredudd ap Rhys Gryg, son of the Lord Rhys, also recognised him as overlord. With the support of the Welsh of the region, he took hold of the Anglo-Norman lordships of south-west Wales up to the outskirts of Pembroke. He then regained Powys Fadog as overlord, but had to seize south Powys from Gruffydd Gwenwynwyn who eventually agreed to give his kingdom to Llywelyn.

With the death of Henry III, his son, Edward I, on returning from the Crusades in 1274, was crowned King of England.

25

Undiplomatically, Llywelyn did not attend the coronation ceremony to pay homage. The relationship between the two was not improved by Llywelyn's continued failure to answer the king's repeated summons for him to pay homage. Llywelyn's proposal to marry Eleanor, the daughter of the late Simon de Montfort, a sworn enemy of Edward I, brought matters to a head, with the king invading Wales in the first of the wars of independence, 1276–77. Llywelyn was defeated and the foundations laid by his grandfather were undermined. Llywelyn Fawr had set about uniting the independent parts of Wales, whilst his grandson adopted a more forceful approach, upsetting Marcher Lords, the forces of the Crown and some Welsh rulers. Llywelyn did not make a conditional surrender and Edward I did not seek to prolong the costly campaign. In the Treaty of Montgomery 1277, the royal hold on Wales was firmly embedded and, although the prince kept his title, it was only as a gesture. The sons of Gruffydd ap Madog kept their rule over northern Powys, and Rhys Fychan continued his hold over Deheubarth but by now independent of Llywelyn. Llywelyn continued to rule over Gwynedd, west of the River Conwy, but the king held Anglesey and the land east of the river, though Anglesey was later given to Llywelyn for his lifetime on terms of feudal tenure. Discontent was widespread, both in west and north Wales, as a result of victimisation on the part of English Crown officials, as well as other injustices which saw Wales yet again involved in a war of independence. The war lasted from 21 March 1282 to June 1283; Llywelyn and his brother Dafydd were slain and the Welsh were defeated.

Victorious Edward I built powerful castles at Conwy and Caernarfon (1283), Harlech (1285) and Beaumaris (1295). Boroughs were created in each of these and also at Criccieth and Bere which, along with Dolwyddelan, were each strengthened and manned with a garrison.

The uprising of 1294–95

Despite the loss of Llywelyn in 1282 and Dafydd in 1283, the Welsh were not daunted. The uprising of 1294–95 was the response of the Welsh to the punitive and unjust regime that benefited the few and impoverished the many. The revolt took place in almost all parts of Wales, commencing towards the end of September 1294 – conveniently when Edward I and his garrisons were due to be in France. The leaders of the rising were Madog in Gwynedd, Maelgwn in Deheubarth, Morgan in Glamorgan and Cynan in Brecon. Edward I brought his army back from France and, on approaching Bangor, he suffered the indignation of having his baggage captured. Much damage occurred during the revolt but within ten months it had come to an end with a Welsh defeat at the Battle of Maes Moydog near present-day Llanfair Caereinion.

Llywelyn Bren and the Despenser dynasty (1314–18)

Following the defeat, Edward I continued to impose heavy fines and there was still discontent amongst the Welsh. On 28 January 1316, Llywelyn Bren, a descendant of Ifor ap Meurig (Ifor Bach), raised his rebellion. It is claimed that 10,000 of his compatriots rose to the cause. The war began with attacks on Caerphilly town and its castle followed by the destruction of castles at Neath, Llantrisant and Kenfig. The walls of Whitchurch were destroyed, as well as the corn mill there and at Machen, Llanfedw and Glyn Rhondda. Four fulling mills were destroyed at Miskin and Rumney; the impact of the rising extending from Rumney to Carmarthen. Llywelyn Bren yielded to an army of superior numbers on 16 March 1316 and was granted a pardon by the king. Two years later however, in 1318, his custodian Hugh Despenser, the new Lord of Glamorgan, put Llywelyn Bren to death and he imprisoned Llywelyn's wife Lleucu and their children. Llywelyn Bren was quartered and his remains buried in Greyfriars House, where Capital Tower is now located in Cardiff city centre. In his will, three books bequeathed by Llywelyn Bren showed that he was a learned man familiar with French and Latin in addition to his native tongue.

Despenser himself was executed in 1326, partly for his treatment of Llywelyn Bren. Following Despenser's execution, Llywelyn's wife Lleucu and their sons were freed (most of their imprisonment had been in Cardiff Castle) and the lands of Senghenydd were restored to them. It is a shame that Despenser is commemorated in Cardiff through Despenser Gardens, but there is nothing to recognise the bravery of Llywelyn Bren.

The Black Plague and Owain Glyndŵr

During the 14th century, notably the years 1347, 1350, 1354, 1361–2, 1369, 1377–83 and 1389–93, countries across Europe suffered terribly from the Black Plague. During this period it is estimated that the population of Wales fell from 300,000 to 200,000 in the wake of the deadly pandemic. In crowded towns and cities, it was not unusual to lose half the population. Certainly, even in the small walled town of Cardiff, the Anglo-Norman inhabitants were more susceptible to the plague than the Welsh who had only limited access to the town and whose dispersed dwellings left them far less vulnerable than those who dwelt within walled towns.

Between the plague and the Edwardian Conquest, the 14th century brought hard times to Wales. The castles, both old and new, were under the control of Anglo-Normans who planted English towns around their fortresses throughout Wales, and the Welsh were forbidden to live in them or carry arms. Soldiers and town burgesses overwhelmed the whole of Wales, the new counties as well as the Marches. The Welsh were denied the right to hold official posts. According to the historian Thomas Tout, Edward I's policy was 'to make Welshmen Englishmen as soon as possible'. At the turn of the 15th century, out of the darkness and despair of the 14th century, Owain Glyndŵr arose and became arguably the most charismatic leader that

Remnants of
Cardiff's town wall

Wales has ever witnessed. He fought for the freedom and advancement of the Welsh people. He pursued proposals for a national parliament, an independent Welsh Church, and the establishment of universities – one in the north and one in the south. One only has to compare Wales with Scotland and the inventions and medical advancements of the latter to see what an advantage having universities since the 14th century has given the Scots.

On 16 September 1400, after a quarrel with powerful Marcher Lord de Grey, Owain with some of his kinsmen carried out a successful attack on Ruthin, the main town within the lordship of de Grey. He followed this with attacks on towns in Clwyd and Powys: Rhuddlan, Flint, Hawarden, Holt, Denbigh, Oswestry and Welshpool, before his army disappeared, guerrilla-style, into the forests and mountains out of reach of the more numerous English army. When the men of Anglesey joined with Glyndŵr, the king called for support from ten English counties. The English parliament was shaken by reports that students were leaving universities to fight alongside Glyndŵr, and Welsh labourers were likewise returning home to fight for their country. At the beginning of 1400 Owain's kinsmen had taken Conwy Castle, whilst he had moved to the south and won a notable battle at Mynydd Hyddgen before moving on to Carmarthen, the domain of Rhys ap Tewdwr, one of his forefathers. In April 1402, Owain captured Lord de Grey and the king was forced to pay a large ransom to free him. Glyndŵr then took the lordship of Maelienydd in Radnorshire, and at the Battle of Bryn Glas he defeated a large English army when Welsh bowmen employed by the English joined with their compatriots. In the battle many English leaders were killed, and Edmund Mortimer, the most important lord of the middle Marches, was captured. The king was unwilling to pay for Mortimer's release. Glyndŵr capitalised on this by blessing the wedding of his daughter Catrin to Mortimer, who ordered his people to join the Welsh cause. With thousands of soldiers in support, Gwynedd and Powys came under Owain's control, together with strong support in Deheubarth.

Owain's power embraced the English counties of the Marcher and Henry Hotspur, Mortimer's brother-in-law, was now at his side. In reaction, the king brought together 100,000 men in three huge armies, aimed at bringing the war to an end. The king's intention however was thwarted by tremendous storms that enabled the guerrilla soldiers to drive them away. Though Hotspur was killed in a battle near Shrewsbury, Glyndŵr's cause went from strength to strength. The king was forced to bring his army to Wales for the fourth time, but he had to turn back without fighting a battle and without weakening Glyndŵr's hold on the land. Owain, with 8,000 at his side, had taken the castles of Llansteffan, Newcastle Emlyn, Dryslwyn and Carreg Cennen. He also received support from French and Breton battleships to attack the castles of Harlech, Caernarfon and Beaumaris in the north and ports in the south. Cardiff was burnt to cinders, including St John's Church, and the castle was taken. The Welsh of the valleys of Gwent and Glamorgan rose in the struggle against a number of enemy towns. The men of Brecknockshire attacked Brecon Castle. The men of Ystrad Tywi acknowledged Glyndŵr as the Prince of Wales. The whole of Wales, with the exception of a few castles, was under his control.

In 1404 the most important of Owain's victories took place. As a result of capturing Aberystwyth and Harlech castles, he won key fortresses and their worth. His family and court were established in Harlech, where they resided for four years. He was served by an able body of civil servants and professional diplomats that included Gruffudd Young, his chancellor, John Trefor, Bishop of Llanelwy, and Llywelyn Byford, soon to be appointed Bishop of Bangor, and he was supported by a keen host of church priests. With them, and in favour of Glyndŵr, stood those of church orders, Franciscans, Austinites, and especially Cistercians, who for years had been supportive of the cause of Wales, its language and culture. One of them was John ap Hywel of Llantarnam, Gwent, a brave and godly man. His life was a good example of the idealism that upheld Owain's cause. He would encourage the zeal of the soldiers before going into battle to defend their homes and their wives and children. He lost his life at the Battle of Pwll Melyn, near Usk, in 1405.

Owain faced a year of mixed fortunes in 1405; his armies were defeated twice in Gwent, one of his sons was killed, and another captured. On the other hand, there was the Triple Contract which divided England and Wales into three parts, for Glyndŵr, Percy and Mortimer. The other great event was the landing of almost 30,000 French soldiers at Milford Haven where Glyndŵr met them with an army of 10,000 men behind him. Haverfordwest was captured, together with the castle and town of Carmarthen, and the allies moved to the east towards Caerleon, then into England, advancing as far as Worcester. From there Glyndŵr retreated to Wales. For the fifth time, the English king invaded Wales with a vast army and once again Welsh weather drove him back.

In 1406 the Triple Contract agreed the previous year between Owain, his son-in-law Edmund Mortimer and Henry Percy to remove Henry IV was destroyed when Percy was killed, and all but a few of the French went home. An attempt by Gruffudd Young, Glyndŵr's chancellor and the future Bishop of Bangor, to make an arrangement with the Scots failed when the English took the Scottish king prisoner. The following year Louis of Orléans, Owain's chief ally in France, was killed and when that country collapsed into disorder, the agreement between those two came to an end.

In 1407 the strength of the English Crown was slowly reasserting itself; the fringe lands of Wales, Gwent, Gower, Pembroke and Anglesey were breaking away, but the core was still solid for Glyndŵr.

In 1408 it was the close and ultimate capture of the Glyndŵr strongholds of Llanbadarn and Harlech which re-established English power in the heart of Wales but, even when castles had fallen to the Crown, the country districts held.

By 1409 the network of government in the principality was functioning once more throughout the Tywi Valley, but the men of Ceredigion, outside the borough of Cardigan, were still in revolt. In the same year, control slowly resumed in south Ceredigion but it was not until 1413 that the northern commotes of Ceredigion were brought into submission.

Harlech Castle was conquered by the English in 1409 and Margaret, Owain's wife, two daughters and three granddaughters, were imprisoned in London. Glyndŵr made his last substantial campaign in 1410 from north Powys, where he still had strength. He attacked the boundary with Shropshire. The day was lost. Key supporters, such as Rhys Ddu, Philip Scudamore and Rhys ap Tudur were gaoled and beheaded as traitors. But Glyndŵr was not totally defeated on the battlefield. He continued to keep large companies of soldiers under his command, and in 1412 he succeeded in taking prisoner the Royalist Dafydd Gam, a member of the Brecknockshire gentry who over the years had been hostile to Glyndŵr.

After 1415 there is no mention of Glyndŵr, apart from the considerable reward that was placed upon his capture. Despite the temptation, he was never betrayed.

Hywel Dda, Llywelyn ein Llyw Olaf, and Owain Glyndŵr are commemorated with marble statutes in Cardiff's City Hall. Also a public house, a stone's throw away from St John's Church which Glyndŵr attacked during his revolt, is named after him.

The Acts of Union and the gentry

Long before the Acts of Union in 1536 and 1543, most of the Welsh landed gentry spoke both English and Welsh, and

33

many were more than prepared to take advantage of the Union legislation that spurred them on to actively discourage the use of Welsh. Yet this was often a process rather than a simple act of the gentry turning their backs on the language. Many gentry families, it is true, gradually adopted English as their only language and others, as the result of arranged marriages with English partners, saw their estates passing into English ownership. On the other hand, not all members of the gentry were unsympathetic to the Welsh language. Sir William Herbert, made first Baron of Cardiff in 1551, spoke Welsh as his first language and insisted on speaking it to his fellow countrymen in the Tudor court. He was born in Ewyas Harold, which was at the time a Welsh-speaking corner of Herefordshire. Later, he became the first Earl of Pembroke of the second creation.[3] Though the Acts of Union had done away with the Marcher Lords, the powers bestowed on the earl placed him in a position of considerable influence. He was the first Welsh speaker based in Cardiff Castle who could exercise such authority, not merely within the lordship of the borough but also throughout Glamorgan. He was made president of the Welsh Council at Ludlow and was involved in a range of matters including affairs of the realm. His powers made him Lord of Glamorgan in all but name. His son, Henry Herbert (*c.*1538–1601), was a patron of industrial enterprise and of English and Welsh literature. His intimate knowledge of Welsh society and love of the language made him, in the words of the distinguished scholar Thomas Wiliems of Trefriw, '*Llygad Holl Gymru*' (the eye of all Wales). In 1576 he restored Cardiff Castle, where he was said to have entertained lavishly. He was succeeded by his son William who was the second earl between 1580 and 1630. On the death of Philip (1584–1650), the fourth earl, the family's Welsh connections weakened. However, during the rule of the Herbert family, there had been a considerable increase in the proportion of Welsh people dwelling in the town. Cardiff Castle was made popular during this time by Welsh bards such as Lewys Dwnn, who praised it in a poem '*Y Gaer fawr a gara fi… lle iachus dyn, lloches deg*' (The large fort that I love… A healthy place for man, a fair haven). The affinity of the family for the language is further witnessed in 1607 when a quarrel between the earl's kinsmen in Herefordshire, not far from Hereford itself, led to a slander case in which the defamatory words were spoken in Welsh.

Sir Edward Stradling, of St Donats, sponsored at great cost Siôn Dafydd Rhys' book of Welsh grammar. Also, William Morgan's classic Welsh Bible, in 1588, brought greater security to the language. Seventy years later, Rhys Prichard's *Canwyll y Cymry* (The Welshman's candle) ran into 52 editions between 1659 and 1820 and its songs were widely read, recited and sung. In general, however, the Anglicising of the gentry in Wales left the people bereft of stable leadership at communal and national levels.

The rise and fall of Anglo-Norman influence

To what extent did Cardiff and its surrounding parishes survive the Anglo-Norman Conquest and thereafter maintain the Welsh language? In the case of the town, to what extent, if any, did the language gain ground? Here one must challenge the age-old assumption that Cardiff has always been an English town, from the building of Fitzhamon's motte-and-bailey between 1093 and 1107 through to the Industrial Revolution and up to the present day.

Certainly, in the days of Anglo-Norman rule, to the monolingual Welsh people of the hills and valleys of Glamorgan and to those in the outlying parishes, undoubtedly the walled town of Cardiff, with its shire hall, law court, gaol, market, biannual fairs, its busy little port and, above all, its Anglo-Norman patois, would have appeared quite alien.

However, by 1578, Rhys ap Meurig from Cottrell in the Vale of Glamorgan seemed to know Cardiff well and had a high opinion of the town:

> The town is very well compacted, beautified with many fine houses
> and large streets... In this town is plenty of good viands to be sold,
> as well for that it is environed with a plentiful and rich soil, as also
> for the continual recourse from it by sea to Bristol and other good
> towns in England.

Following the Act of Union in 1536, Cardiff had become
a county town and became a legal and administrative centre.
John Speed's map of 1610 shows Cardiff to be split into two
parishes, St Mary's in the south and St John's in the north and,
by that time, the town is estimated to be populated by around
a thousand people.

Welsh speakers were certainly rare within the town walls
in the first 250 years after the arrival of the Anglo-Normans.
They were bent on extending their conquests, and the 'Dublin
list' of 1172–1230 catalogues the names of 36 soldiers who had
gone from Cardiff in 1169 to Ireland in the company of Earl
Richard FitzGilbert Striguil (better known as Strongbow). The
list consists mainly of French names, with occasional English

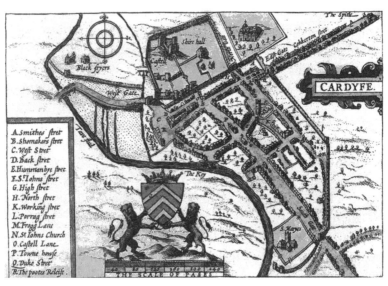

John Speed's map of Cardiff, 1610
© Glamorgan Archives

ones reflecting the strong Anglo-Norman coalition. Some of the names stemmed from the areas in Glamorgan where the Normans had acquired land: Hugh de Roth (Roath), Henry de Lancarvan (Llancarfan), Phillip de Marcross (Marcroes) and Thomas Penarth. It is surprising that no Welsh names appear on this list, considering the popularity in Ireland of the surname 'Walsh', derived from the many Welsh mercenaries who are said to have assisted Strongbow in his conquest of Leinster on the death of the Irish King Dermot in 1171.

Very scarce indeed were the Welsh who dwelt inside Cardiff's walled town, and in the hundred years from 1299 to 1399, there are only nine Welsh names amongst those registered as inhabitants: namely Aron ap Howel (1299), Howel ap Howel (1331), Morgan Lloyd (1340), Morgan de Ffeirwater (1348), John ap Rees (1376), William Walsh (1376), Ieuan Percy (1376), William ap Ieuan ap Howel (1393), and William David (1398). It would seem useful for the Anglo-Normans to have had a bilingual Welshman within the town walls to act as a translator and as a general conduit with the native Welsh who dwelt nearby.

Roath, Rumney and Leckwith

With their manorial duties, and their proximity to the town, Roath, Rumney and Leckwith appear to have been dominated by the Anglo-Normans up to the beginning of the 15th century. However, by the 16th century and through to the middle of the 19th century, Welsh had been restored as the language of these three parishes.

The other parishes and the Welsh language

The evidence from the place-names and surnames of the other 11 parishes suggests that the Welsh language had been prevalent before and throughout the years of Anglo-Norman rule and, in some cases, even up to the second half of the 19th century and beyond. In the parishes of Llanedeyrn, Pentyrch,

37

Lisvane, Radyr and St Mellons, Welsh was still the predominant language up to the turn of the 20th century. In the parishes of Llandaff, Llanishen, Whitchurch, Caerau, St Fagans and Michaelston-super-Ely, the language began to retreat in the second half of the 19th century.

Population of the town and its surrounding parishes, 1670–1851

Year	1670[4]	1801	1811	1821	1831	1841	1851
Cardiff	1,515	1,870	2,457	3,521	6,187	10,077	18,351
Llandaff	831	860	960	1,138	1,299	1,276	1,821
Roath	314	236	211	269	272	298	312
Llanedeyrn	432	301	263	348	315	354	338
Llanishen	347	329	307	360	393	418	388
Lisvane	295	221	231	230	253	207	220
Whitchurch	200	696	997	972	1,184	1,376	1,661
Pentyrch	160	470	475	747	926	1,258	1,599
Radyr	169	196	106	128	227	279	417
Caerau	81	65	43	69	77	80	87
Michaelston	95	53	43	53	60	54	48
St Fagans	336	365	397	510	446	424	515
Rumney	320	235	237	255	264	305	308
St Mellons	558	451	515	551	564	613	637
Total	**5,653**	**6,348**	**7,242**	**9,151**	**12,467**	**17,019**	**26,702**

Cardiff town's population in 1670 was 1,515, only a quarter of that of the combined 13 parishes, namely those which now form a part of the capital city.[5]

CHAPTER 2

What's in a Name?

Welsh and Anglo-Norman surnames

By the 13th century, half the people of England had fixed surnames and this rose to 75% by the first quarter of the 14th century. As a result of establishing surnames in England, many local surnames such as Dale, Marsh and Kent; trade names such as Smith, Brewer and Baker; nicknames such as Armstrong, Goodfellow and Brown became common surnames. In addition to these, many patronymic names were created, e.g. Robinson, Johnson and Wilson. Whereas a variety of surnames were being adopted in England, similar names in Wales changed from generation to generation. The process of adopting a surname as in England, as opposed to retaining the Welsh tradition of patronymics, often took place over three generations. For example, a great-grandfather known as John ap Howell would drop the 'ap', and the grandfather would becomes Rhys Howell; the father and subsequent generations would adopt the genitive 's', making Howells the fixed family surname. Not infrequently, however, the genitive 's' was not adopted, so that one branch of a family had the surname Griffiths for example, whilst their cousins would have adopted the surname Griffith. Sometimes the adoption of a different or new surname would occur, so Dafydd ap Rosser would become Dafydd Prosser, or Richard ab Owen became Richard Bowen. Welsh surnames were established gradually over the period 1500 to 1800, with those dwelling in Anglo-Norman towns or those having moved to England taking fixed surnames earlier than those living in Welsh rural areas who tended to delay the move towards the adoption of a permanent surname. A local example of the change in surname would be the Pritchard family of Llancaiach Fawr who held land and houses in Cardiff. The manor house of Llancaiach Fawr was built in the mid 15th century by a Dafydd ap Richard. His grandson, who became the Governor of Cardiff during the Royalist siege of the civil war in February 1646, was known as Edward Prichard.

Analysing the numbers of Welsh and Anglo-Normans in the Cardiff area

In 1301 the Provost of Rumney presented his account in which eight inhabitants are named, and from this it can be seen that seven have Anglo-Norman names and one has a Welsh name. By 1316 the Minister of Accounts list for Roath and Rumney shows the following eight names: Gronow ap Rosser, David ap Llewelyn, David Pilgrym, John Giffard, Adam Godman, John Snovgood, John Philip and John Daye. Clearly, the third, fourth, fifth and sixth names are of Anglo-Norman origin, whilst the first and second names are traditional Welsh patronymics. The seventh and eighth names are most likely in the middle of the process of change, where the first generation was probably known as John ap Philip, his son became John Philip, and by the third generation we would have John Philips. Likewise, John ap Daye (Dai) would have turned into John Daye (Dai) then John David or Davies. This brief list suggests a population in Roath and Rumney that is evenly divided between the Welsh and Anglo-Normans at the beginning of the 14th century.

The list alone, however, is too short for one to be conclusive about the growth of the Welsh element in the parishes of Roath and Rumney. But later, in 1492, the Minister of Accounts list for Roath includes 34 names, of which 18 are Welsh, 14 are English and two could be either Welsh or English. The list includes five Welsh patronymics: Ieuan ap Jac, David ap Jankyn, David ap Hoel (Hywel), Richard ap Guillim Loid (Richard Gwilym Lloyd) and Morgan ap John Gwyn.

In 1492 the Minister of Accounts list for Leckwith lists 11 names, of which six are Welsh, three are English and two that could be either. It appears that the Welsh in Leckwith were gradually reinhabiting the lands previously in the hands of the Anglo-Normans.

The Minister of Accounts list for 1492 for the Cardiff Borough lists 38 names: 23 English, 13 Welsh and two that could be either. The Cardiff list includes the following names which emphasise the growing Welsh presence in the town compared to the previous century: patronymic names – Thomas ap David, John ap Rees and Ieuan ap Thomas; nicknames – William Coys (coes = leg) and Isabel Wynne (wyn = fair); and trade names – Llywelyn Bochor (butcher) and Ieuan Baker. The list also includes three names where the Welsh 'ap' has been dropped but the genitive 's' not yet added – John Hugh, William Philip, and Margaret Edward. One surname on the list is taken from a dwelling place, John Cogan, whereas the name Richard Meuric is an example of a surname surviving without the addition of the genitive 's', with Meuric or Meyrick most likely becoming the fixed surname for future generations of that family.[6]

The Minister of Accounts list for Radyr, Pentyrch and Whitchurch in 1492 shows a dominance of Welsh names, and similarly the list for Roath in the same year shows that the Welsh by then were a majority, with native names being 53% of the total.

Amongst the names in the lists for the walled town in 1492 appears the name Robert Jones, who possibly was the first Welshman in Cardiff to have had a fixed surname. No Welsh patronymic names are encountered in the lists for the town, but that is not to say that all the names had become fixed: John Hugh, Margaret Edward, William Philip and John Thomas were likely to be names which would have the genitive 's' added maybe in the next generation, thus becoming John Hughes, Margaret Edwards, William Philips, whilst the name John Thomas, already ending in an 's', would remain unchanged.

The Bailey's Accounts for Cardiff Borough and Roath listed 208 names in 1542–43. Of the names, 123 were English (59%), 80 were Welsh (38.5%), and seven (2.5%) could have been English or Welsh.

The 1550 List of Tenants of St John's and St Mary's parishes show more Welsh names than English:

Table: List of tenants of St John's and St Mary's parishes, 1550

Number of Names	Number of Welsh Names	Number of English Names
61	32	29

In the 16th-century tenants' list for the town, there are names such as Lewis Hoell (Hywel), otherwise Ffletcher, and also Lewis Powell Ffletcher. This is almost certainly the same person where Lewis ap Howel Ffletcher becomes Lewis Powel Ffletcher, alias Lewis Howel Ffletcher. This example shows how flexible surnames were in Cardiff at that time. Here are some other examples of nicknames, local surnames and trade names of this period, and all it would seem, as yet, not having permanent surnames:

Table: Some surnames in Cardiff, 1583–94

1583	John Thomas Bengoh [Bengough] = John Red Head
1583	Lewis Jenkyns, alias Tanner
1584	Lewis Thomas, alias Taylor
1587	John Vine [main > Fain] = thin
1590	David ab Owen, Weaver
1591	Richard Langmeade [Landmeade, land in Adamsdown]
1594	Walter Philip, otherwise Cooke, Yeoman
1594	Richard William, otherwise Bushe
1594	Thomas Comyn

By 1542, the Minister of Accounts list for Roath has 44 names, of which 66% are Welsh, 27% are English and some 7% are names that could be either Welsh or English; a 13% increase in Welsh names in Roath since 1492.

Around 1578, there is a list of 59 freeholders, all with Welsh names, covering the parishes of Llandaff, Roath, Caerau, Whitchurch, Llanishen, Lisvane, and Llanedeyrn.

Welsh surnames in Cardiff, 1600-99

By the second half of the 17th century, all but one Welsh surnames in Cardiff appear without the prefix 'ap' or 'ab'. Furthermore, many nicknames and trade names have been displaced by patronymic surnames terminating in the genitive 's', such as Jones and Williams, whilst a large number of surnames, such as Evan, Howell and Griffith appear as yet without the genitive 's'. According to H.B. Guppy, an authority on surnames, Williams was 15 times more common in south Wales in 1890 than in Somerset.

Table: Sample of surnames in Cardiff, 1444–1806

Roath, 1670/71	The local tax list	64 names	61 Welsh	3 English
Llanedeyrn, 1670/71	Hearth tax list	90 names	81 Welsh	9 English
Radyr, 1666	Rent list	6 names	5 Welsh	1 English
St Fagans, 1666	Rent list	10 names	10 Welsh	0 English
Total		**170 names**	**157 Welsh**	**13 English**
Cardiff Borough, 1666	Manorial records of rents due	225 names	135 Welsh	90 English
The Cordwainers of Cardiff (Shoemakers), 1444–1650	List of membership	34 names	17 Welsh	17 English
The Cordwainers of Cardiff, 1651–1806	List of membership	129 names	73 Welsh	56 English

The growth of the Welsh presence within the town is further confirmed by the 1666 List of Tenants that totalled 232 names, of which 152 (65.5%) were Welsh and 80 (34.5%) were English.[7] The Welsh predominance in the surrounding parishes was even more considerable. By 1666, the names of the tenants of Cardiff town had lost a lot of the colour of the various names of the previous century. However, there remained the occasional nickname, such as Edward Landick (*glân a theg*, which means handsome) and Mary Gwyn, or Mary White; one old Welsh surname, James ab Evan; and two local names, John Bembrick (Pembroke) and Ann Vynor (Faenor). By then Welsh-based long-established English surnames such as Bassett, Gibbon and Stradling are placed amongst the Welsh names.

Welsh surnames in Cardiff, 1700–1835

Gradually, during the 18th and early 19th centuries, most surnames saw the addition of the genitive 's', becoming Evans, Howells and Griffiths etc. However, older Welsh surnames such as Llywelyn, Morgan and Rhys retained their traditional forms. The table below shows that by the mid 18th century Welsh names were dominant in the town, in stark contrast to the nine only Welsh names between 1299 and 1399. A list of parishioners of the town for the period 1736–72 show that three-quarters have Welsh surnames. The figure increases to 90% in the surrounding parishes. Clearly, Cardiff was once again a Welsh town, as is shown in the table below.

Table: People on St John's parish register, 1736–72

Number of names	Welsh Names	English Names
150	115 (77%)	35 (23%)

Slander cases, 1710–1810

Another substantial source of information regarding names within the town of Cardiff and the surrounding parishes can be found amongst the records of slander cases that largely took place between 1710 and 1810. The evidence below has been divided into three periods: 1710–40, 1741–70 and 1771–1810. The names include the complainants, the defendants, and those giving evidence. This source also reveals the slanderous words recorded in the language used, i.e. Welsh or English. During the period 1700–1800, a total of 750 slander cases were held around Glamorgan and Gwent, with 475 in Welsh and 275 in English. Chapter three explores how the slander cases reveal the extent of the use of the two languages in the town and parishes during this period.

Table: Names in slander cases in Cardiff, 1710–1810

Years	Total names	Welsh names	English names
1710–1740	169	126 (74.5%)	43 (25.5%)
1741–1770	90	76 (84.5%)	14 (15.5%)
1771–1810	64	56 (87.5%)	8 (12.5%)
Total	**323**	**258 (79.9%)**	**65 (20.1%)**

The above slander cases, with a total of 323 names, shows again a clear growth in the Welsh presence between 1710 and 1810, from 74.5% Welsh names to 87.5%.

At this time the following Nonconformist chapels were established in the town: the Welsh- and English-language Wesleyan chapel in 1794, Bethany Baptist in 1804, Tabernacl Welsh Baptist in 1813, and Ebeneser Welsh Independent in 1826. A review of their registers between 1799 and 1837 shows a similar finding to the slander cases, in that 85% of the names were Welsh.

Table: Names on registers of Nonconformist chapels in Cardiff, 1799–1837

Total names	Welsh names	English names
551	467 (85%)	84 (15%)

Reasons for the increase of the Welsh presence in Cardiff

In 1801, when the population of Cardiff was enumerated for the first time, Welsh was the main language spoken by the inhabitants of the town and surrounding parishes. The shape of the town was similar to when John Speed mapped it in 1610. There are a number of contributory factors leading to the growth of the Welsh presence within both the town and the surrounding parishes.

Firstly, the uprising of Llywelyn Bren in 1316 resulted in long-standing damage and huge costs over a wide area that would have made dwelling in the walled town less attractive.

Secondly, the outbreaks of the plague in the 14th century, especially those of 1361 and 1369, are likely to have drastically decreased the Anglo-Norman population within the town, and consequently caused a considerable loss of revenue.

Thirdly, and even more irreversible, was the impact of Owain Glyndŵr's attack on the town when the Welsh forces broke through the West Gate and wrought great destruction on the castle and the dwellings. The Anglo-Normans were forced to raise additional taxes for almost a hundred years in order to repair the extensive damage. Seemingly, the repairs were not completed even then, as Henry Herbert is said to have carried out restoration of the castle in 1576.

Fourthly, the Acts of Union of 1536 and 1543 gave the Welsh the freedom to dwell within walled towns.

Fifthly, as previously mentioned, the Herbert family who were supportive of the Welsh language were the Barons of Cardiff from the middle of the 15th century onwards.

Finally, the surrounding parishes had an estimated combined population in 1670 of 4,200, almost threefold that of the town with its estimated population of 1,515. The first official census of 1801 shows that the total population of the two areas was 6,432, with the population of the town being only 1,870, compared to 4,562 in the parishes. Evidence suggests that most of the parishes remained overwhelmingly

Welsh through the Norman period and this had an eventual effect on the town.

Conclusion

Counting separately Anglo-Norman and Welsh personal names is not a perfect means of gauging with exactitude the numbers of each group. However, all in all, the considerable evidence studied provides a reasonable basis upon which to assert that over the period from 1550 to 1850, the Welsh population was numerically predominant. Moreover, the number of people with Welsh surnames within the surrounding parishes was considerably larger than the number of people with Anglo-Norman surnames living within the same parishes. This is supported by what was happening in the Vale of Glamorgan at the time. An anonymous scribe, writing in the *Seren Gomer* weekly newspaper in 1824, outlined the rapidity of the change from English to Welsh in the area surrounding Llantwit Major: 'Whereas English had been the only language understood here 50 or 60 years ago, it is just as fruitful, comforting and worthy now as was at that time and rather more so that Welsh is now the common language of the people.' However, as we will see in chapters seven and eight, the language position changed quickly again in the opposite direction.

*

What's in a place-name?

A further investigation on the position of the Welsh language in Cardiff is made through looking at place-names in the town and surrounding parishes. The intention here is not to make a thorough study of the origin and development of individual place-names, such as carried out by Gwynedd O. Pierce in his books, *The Place-names of Dinas Powys Hundred* and *Place-names in Glamorgan*, or the work of R.J. Thomas on the commote of Miskin. Rather, the aim is to study the place-names of Cardiff and its surrounding parishes with a view to bringing together evidence of the use of Welsh and English during the period 1100 to 1851. The areas include place-names within the walled town of Cardiff, those parts of the borough that lay outside the walls, and the various parishes that by today form a part of the city. It concentrates on the place-names of farms, houses, roads, fields and structures of relevance to this study from the 12th century to the mid 19th century.

There are 12 Cardiff place-names noted by J. Hobson Mathews, the town's archivist in the late 20th century, prior to 1350. Nine are within the walled town: Capella S. Pirani (1188), Cabelle Strete (13th century), Hundemanby (1270), Womanby Street and Sallyuggyswere (both 1316), Shipmanstrete (1321), Alta Strata de Kaerdif (1331), Bothe-halle (1331) and Crokarton (1348). The other four are boundary names of the Liberties of Cardiff Borough cited in the Municipal Charter of 1340, namely Appledore, Bradstrem, Paynescros and the Cross near the Friars Preachers or Black Friars. However, it is likely that at this time Welsh place-names were used in the surrounding parishes and later slowly introduced into the town and Roath.

Table A: Cardiff place-names, 1110–1492

Area / Town	Total Place-names	Total Welsh Place-names	% Welsh Place-names	Total English Place-names	% English Place-names
Canton	2	0	0%	2	100%
Leckwith	30	0	0%	30	100%
Llanedeyrn	2	2	100%	0	0%
Roath	51	4	8%	47	92%
Rumney	7	5	71.5%	2	28.5%
Town	25	5	20%	20	80%
Whitchurch	10	8	80%	2	20%
Totals	**127**	**24**	**19%**	**103**	**81%**

The parishes of Roath and Leckwith, together with the town, show a predominance of Anglo-Norman place-names up to 1492. On the other hand, the 19 combined place-names from the parishes of Whitchurch, Llanedeyrn and Rumney reveal 79% Welsh place-names as against 21% Anglo-Norman place-names. Though the quantity of evidence is not very extensive, it serves to undermine a preconceived picture of a coastal English area stretching from Rumney and Roath, through the town and the hamlet of Canton, to Leckwith. It seems reasonable to assume that this was not in fact the case, as a search of the hamlet of Canton reveals only two Anglo-Norman place-names. The hamlet's location within Llandaff sets it apart from the manorial arrangements for Roath and Leckwith.

When the Crown freed the Bishop of Llandaff from allegiance to the Lord of Cardiff in 1300, bishops gained a significant measure of independence from the castle. Llandaff was to some extent a buffer zone, being neither part of an Englishry nor a Welshry. As noted in the table above, there are two dated place-names for Canton. These are Sudcroft in 1290 and the Grange of the Moor. During the 13th century, the abbey of Margam established a grange on the bishop's land that came to be known as the Grange of the Moor. A survey of the property took place in 1312, suggesting that a building then existed.

Table B: Cardiff place-names, 1500–1700

Area	Total Place-names	Total Welsh Place-names	% Welsh Place-names	Total English Place-names	% English Place-names
Canton and Grange	15	12	80%	3	20%
Leckwith	15	2	13%	13	87%
Llandaff	97	78	80%	19	20%
Roath	61	12	20%	49	80%
Rumney	1	1	100%	0	0%
St Fagans	6	6	100%	0	0%
Town	76	18	24%	58	76%
Total	**271**	**129**	**48%**	**142**	**52%**

The most significant statistic in the table above is the large number of Welsh place-names in Llandaff, with 80% of place-names being Welsh. Similarly, in stark contrast to the previous table, 80% of the place-names in Canton (including Grange) were Welsh. Whilst the Leckwith search produced 30 place-names for 1110–1492 (see Table A), none of which were Welsh, this number was halved to 15 during 1500–1700 but two were Welsh. Though Rumney yielded only one place-name in the 1500–1700 search, the fact that it was Welsh illustrates a continued decline in the Anglo-Norman presence as witnessed in Table A. The 100% of Welsh place-names in St Fagans further strengthens the supposition that only Roath and Leckwith had undergone a period of extensive Anglicisation during the Anglo-Norman period along with that of the town. Moreover, both the town and Roath witnessed increased percentages of Welsh place-names of 24% and 20% respectively. From 1550 the total percentage of Welsh place-names for the whole area had increased from 21% to 72%.

Table C: Place-names in manors of Cardiff, 1600–1702

Area	No. of Place-names	No. of Welsh Place-names	% of Welsh Place-names	No. of English Place-names	% of English Place-names
Lisvane	7	7	100%	0	0%
Llandaff	42	33	79%	9	21%
Llanedeyrn	20	20	100%	0	0%
Llys-tal-y-bont	40	40	100%	0	0%
Pentyrch	31	30	97%	3	3%
Roath Keynsham	76	73	96%	3	4%
St Fagans	40	40	100%	0	0%
Town	111	33	30%	78	70%
Total	**367**	**276**	**75%**	**93**	**25%**

Again, to support the findings of the previous table, Table C also shows the predominance of Welsh place-names in manors outside of the town between 1600 and 1702.

Up to the beginning of the 18th century, both place-names and the personal names of the population show an increase in the Welsh presence in the town and a strong continual existence in most of the surrounding parishes.

Street names and other place-names

Most Welsh towns were originally built as Anglo-Norman settlements and it is notable that street names are, or have been, almost exclusively English, even where the Welsh language is at its strongest. It is only since the latter decades of the 20th century that Welsh or bilingual signs have become increasingly common. Under the Acts of Union 1536 and 1543, the law and order of the land insisted that there be officials with the ability to speak English. The Acts of Union forbade anyone from holding governmental office if they were unable 'to use and exercise the speech or language of English'. Therefore, it is not surprising that place-names devised by governmental officials would remain English. Nonetheless, as the Welsh language in Cardiff continued to grow, alternative place-names for streets, public houses, town gates, the port quay and other structures such as those along the canal wharfs began to appear:

- Hewl y Cawl, in place of Wharton Street (1713, 1737)
- Blunch Gate (Welsh pronunciation), in place of Blounts Yate (1750)
- Cae Clawdy, in place of the Poorhouse Field (1814)
- Sarn Fidfoel (road of the bare hedge), in place of North Road (c.1700)
- Cae'r Fidfoel (field of the bare hedge), on the site of present Civic Centre (1714, 1749)
- Cae Pwdwr, defiled field in Hewl Plwca – today's City Road (1728, 1761, 1788)

- Cae Twc, in place of Tucking Field on Maendy Farm (1637, 1778, 1783)
- Carreg Pica, a pointed stone look-out near the castle (1719, 1797, 1833)
- Hewl Plwca, became Castle Road in 1874 and City Road in 1905 (1777)
- Cwchmoel, name of Cardiff Gaol (Norman French – Cockmarel) (1555, 1578)
- Pwll Halog, defiled pool where Merthyr Road and Hewl Plwca met roads renamed Albany and City in the 20th century (1737)
- Cae Pwdwr, rotten field – Gallows Pit was sited nearby (1750, 1803)
- Tŷ Coch (Red House), later Cardiff Arms, near today's Angel Hotel
- Porth Llongau, in place of Shipgate/Southgate
- Porth Dŵr, in place of Water Gate
- Porth Meisgyn, in place of West Gate
- Porth Senghennydd, in place of North Gate
- Porth Crocerton, in place of East Gate
- Gwlat (Welsh pronunciation), in place of Gullate (1800, 1840)
- Tŷ Llwyd, in place of the Grey House
- Tri-chwarter Caerdydd, for Three-quarters of an acre, near Love Lane in town
- Maendy (1724)
- Maendy Bach (1783)
- Plas Newydd, near River Taff (1536–9)
- Plasnewydd, in High Street (c.1600)
- Tir Ceiliog, now part of Cathays Cemetery (1776, 1801)
- Llwyn-y-pia farm, between Cathays Cemetery and Pen-y-waun (1850)
- Tir Derwen Deg, pub in Angel Street (1848)

- Dic y Fuwch Goch – landlord of the Red Cow (1776, 1792)
- Y Brenin, King's Castle, Canton (1710, 1796, 1823)
- Cae'r Castell, a field surrounding King's Castle
- William Ceiliog Du – landlord of the Black Cock (1774)
- Pentwyn House (1782)
- Crwys Bychan (c.1540)
- Plasturton (1745)
- Llys Talybont (1751)
- Pontcanna (1719, 1731)
- Y Waun Ddyfal (1801)
- Stafell Wen, Stafell yr Oged (Rhys Meurig)
- Hilla Uchaf a Hilla Isaf (Rhys Meurig)
- Tŷ'n yr ardd, later part of Charles Street (c.1850)
- Naw erw duon
- Pum Erw Tir James
- Cae'r Cornel
- Dwy erw'r Fair
- Cae Tai Llwydon
- Tŷ Wyndham Lewis

Estate maps and tithe maps, 1700–1845

Estate maps provide us with evidence of place-names from the earlier part of this period, whilst the tithe maps cover the largely rural areas of the 15 parishes from around 1839 to 1845. The study concentrates on the field names in use at the time, and seeks to determine whether or not the Welsh language had displaced English in all or some of the parishes. The evidence suggests that Welsh field names in Cardiff were generally formed by using the relevant number of acres covered by a field, along with some other description. For example:

- Erw y Clochdy (Bellhouse acre)
- Erw y Gro (Sandy acre)

- Dwy erw a hanner (Two and a half acres)
- Tair Erw Penfaen (Three capstone acres)
- Pedair Erw Drain Duon (Four blackthorn acres)
- Pum Erw Dyrus (Five thorny acres)
- Wecherw Duon (Six black acres)
- Saith Erw Melyn (Seven Yellow Acres)
- Wyth Erw y Sblot Isha (Lower Splott Eight Acres)
- Naw Erw (Nine Acres)
- Deg Erw hir (Ten Long Acres)
- Gwaun y Sblot Isha (Lower Splott Meadow)
- Tir y Sbitl (Spittal Land)
- Tir Newydd (New Land)
- Tir Siwsan (Susan's Land)
- Tri Chwarter Caerdydd (Cardiff's Three-quarters of an acre)
- Gwaun Sion Hywel (Sion Hywel's meadow)

Table: Field names from estate, tithe and town maps, 1700–1849

| Areas | Estate maps c.1777 | | Tithe maps c.1840/45 | | |
	Number of names	Welsh names	Number of names	Welsh names	Total % of Welsh names
Caerau	13	12	139	129	93%
Canton	48	48	–	–	100%
Llandaff	185	156	606	446	76%
Llanedeyrn	89	83	652	610	94%
Llanishen	140	127	28	25	90%
Lisvane	80	80	37	32	96%
Michaelston-super-Ely	73	71	70	56	89%
Pentyrch	–	–	823	770	94%
Radyr	92	77	39	31	82%
Roath	–	–	292	160	55%
Rumney	57	45	38	25	74%
Splott (Tredegar Estate)	50	49	–	–	98%

St Fagans	126	106	137	129	89%
St John's (rural)	39	25	32	16	58%
St Mary's (rural)	7	6	–	–	86%
St Mellons	110	107	37	36	97%
Whitchurch	–	–	535	460	86%
Total	**1,109**	**992**	**3,467**	**2,925**	**86%**

The information from the tithe maps from 1839 until 1845 includes over 3,400 field names and so provides a considerable collection of evidence. Both sets of maps are marked out, numbered, and the fields named. However, there is a notable lack of consistency in the method of recording the details on either set of maps. For example, the numbers on the tithe map for Llandaff range from one to 1,210, but only 834 of them are linked to field names, whilst the remaining 376 are either blank or carry bare descriptions such as 'pasture', 'waste', 'house and gardens' and 'road to Cardiff'. For the purposes of this work the focus on the estate and tithe maps is on field names alone, and are divided into Welsh-language or English-language categories.

Corresponding field names on the estate and tithe maps can be compared, and translations detected when the original Welsh field names on an estate map have been translated into English. R.J. Thomas, in his study of the manors of St Fagans, draws attention to the habit of those who had carried out the tithe survey of the Plymouth Estate of translating Welsh field names into English. He notes, 'In the Survey of the Manors of St. Ffagans... in English only are the field names, even though it is certain that the largest part of them are translations from Welsh field names.' Frequently this can be confirmed by comparing tithe map entries with those of estate maps covering parts of the same area. Wherever R.J. Thomas identifies a translation, I have counted the names as such. The same practice has been carried out with the fields of the Plymouth Estate in Radyr. Moreover, in Roath, comparing

the map of the Tredegar Estate for Splott in 1777 with the
Roath tithe map for Splott in 1840 illustrates further instances
of translation from Welsh to English.

Table: Comparing Tredegar Estate map and Roath tithe map

Field number	Tredegar Estate (Splott, 1777)	Roath tithe map (Splott, 1840)
No. 32	Cae Pica[8]	Cae Pica
No. 33	Seithr Bach	The Seven Acres
No. 34	Nawer y Botoms	The Seventeen Acres
No. 35	Wyther y Botwms	
Nos 20, 21, 22	Tir newydd	The Thirty Acres
No. 25	Gwaun y Sblot Isha	The Lower Splott Meadow
No. 15	Erw y Beam	
	Seither y Glwyd	The Fifteen Acres
	Pedair Erw y Draen Duon	
No. 18	Erw'r Delyn	
No. 19	Dwy erw y bwlch	Land on the Moors
No. 14	Pumerw Dyrus	
No. 44	Pedar Erw Llewelyn	Four Acres
No. 41	Wyther y Lancros	The Eight Acres
No. 43	Wyther y Winch	The Eight Acres

Of the 50 Welsh field names that dominate the Tredegar
Estate map (Splott, 1777), more than half of them had been
translated or displaced by English names when the Roath tithe
map of 1844 was drawn up. The opening of the Bute East Dock
in 1839 and the Taff Vale Railway in 1841 boosted Splott's
potential for further development and, undoubtedly, many
fields were merged and renamed as the expansion of the town
grew apace.

The place-names of Caerau also presented a situation
where clearly Welsh place-names on the estate map had been
translated to English names on the tithe map.

Table: Comparing the Caerau Estate map and tithe map

Field number	Sweldon Estate map	Sweldon tithe map
No. 14	Wech Erw and Berllan	The six acres and Cae Berllan (one translated, the other not)
No. 92	Erw dan y coed	Acre under wood

Around 89.5% of the 1,007 field names gathered from the estate maps and spread over the 15 parishes were Welsh. Likewise, 84.5% of the 3,433 field names gathered from the tithe maps and spread over the 15 parishes were Welsh, showing strong evidence of the Welsh language in Cardiff between 1700 and 1845.

Place-names on estate maps, 1766–1819

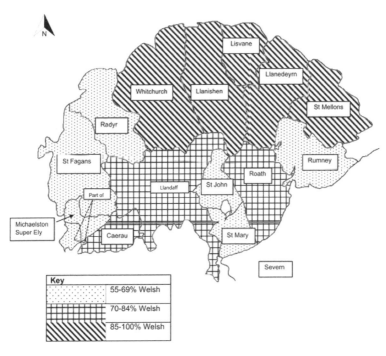

CHAPTER 3

Gossip, Slander and Scandal: The inns (and outs) of Cardiff

THIS CHAPTER REVEALS a different side to the Welsh speakers of Cardiff to what has become a popular belief, that they were respectable, middle class and chapelgoing. It shows the popularity of public houses in Cardiff, their links to the Welsh language and, often following a number of alcoholic drinks, how prevalent was the use of that language in slander cases.

In 1792, after receiving notice that they should renew their licenses for the year, no fewer than 32 Cardiff licensees paid a fee of £10 each, together with sureties of a further £10, binding them to keep good order and to ensure that they would not allow any unlawful games to be played within their respective premises. By 1812, however, with the population now 2,500, there were no fewer than 40 public houses in the town. Despite being around the same size as Aberystwyth, Cardiff was not an insignificant centre. On market days, Wednesdays and Saturdays, many of the inhabitants of the surrounding parishes would make the journey on foot to visit the market to trade their goods and doubtless enjoy a glass or two of beer. For those who owned a horse, the temptation to linger late at an inn could sometimes lead to a fatal accident. Apparently, farmers would frequently be thrown from their horses when returning drunk from the market, especially when attempting to cross a river, be it the Taff, the Rhymney, or the Ely.

The town's nearest equivalent to rugby internationals or Eisteddfodau were the two annual fairs, each lasting a fortnight, one starting on the eve of St John the Baptist (24 June) and the other on the Feast of the Nativity of St Mary (8 September). Llandaff also held two annual fairs, on Teilo's anniversary on 9 February, and the Whitsun fair on Whit Monday. The fairs attracted people from near and far: traders, packmen and entertainers who would pay fees and tolls to have the right to set up their stalls. It was these consistent events, drawing in large numbers from outside, that enabled the town, despite its small population, to sustain up to 40 public houses from time to time. The decline of the Anglo-Norman presence seems to have been more than counterbalanced by the growing movement of the Welsh from the hinterland to the Vale of Glamorgan. As previously mentioned, this migration was accelerated by the Acts of Union 1536 and 1543 which gave the Welsh access to the town. Then there was also the rule of the Herbert dynasty from 1550 to 1700.

When studying the place-names of the town from 1700 to 1835, the names of public houses, akin to those of street names, were invariably English. Once an inn had been licensed, its name would remain, and it is likely that for every Llew Coch there would be at least a dozen Red Lions. Yet, there is evidence showing that official names, be they for streets or public houses, often had an alias or nickname. For example, it is recorded that the innkeeper of the King's Head from 1732 to 1737, on the boundary of St John's and the hamlet of Canton, was commonly known as 'Y Brenin', which means the king in English. The estate map covering that area shows that the inn was situated on Cae'r Brenin, meaning the King's Field. Likewise, the licensee of the Red Cow in Womanby Street was known as 'Dic y Fuwch' (1731), in English, Dick the Cow[9]. William of the Black Cock was commonly known as 'William y

Ceiliog Du' (1744). Other inns known by both their Welsh and English names were Y Ddrag ag Oged (1792), alias The Plough and Harrow, and Y Tŷ Coch (1710, 1731, 1777, 1788), alias The Red House[10].

The Glove and Shears stood on the corner of today's Kingsway and the now long-demolished side of Duke Street (1792). The front wall of the inn faced along the Running Camp (later Queen Street), and bore a sign for many years until the beginning of the 20th century declaring: '*Cymry a Chymraeg tu fewn*' (Welsh people and Welsh within).

Some public houses are remembered for historical reasons, such as the Cross Keys (1792, 1806), a public house just outside the town wall at the western end of Crocerton Street on the corner of the lane that ran alongside the canal tunnel. Around Christmas 1832, Cymdeithas Cymreigyddion Caerdaf was formed to promote local Eisteddfodau. The following November, its members met in the Cross Keys and, after a glass or two, marched to the Tabernacl Welsh Baptist chapel on The Hayes where a sermon was given. They then returned to the Cross Keys for dinner (and probably another glass or two!) before gathering in Bethany Baptist chapel at the St Mary Street end of Hewl y Cawl (Wharton Street) where the proceedings of the Eisteddfod were held. Annual Eisteddfodau followed thereafter, the second being held in the Guild Hall in 1834, the fourth being held at the Angel Tavern in 1837, and returning to the Guild Hall in 1839.

The 1834 Eisteddfod in the Guild Hall was opened by Taliesin ab Iolo, the son of Iolo Morganwg. Lady Llanover won a ring worth ten guineas for an essay on the importance of maintaining the Welsh language and Welsh costumes. Another winner was 14-year-old Brinley Richards, who later composed 'God Bless the Prince of Wales' (an anthem which thankfully has been largely forgotten but was popular during my childhood in Cardiff). The Eisteddfodau were not always vehicles for promoting the Welsh language. A competition for a prize of £3 at the 1864 Eisteddfod in the Temperance Hall, Wood Street, was an essay on the title, 'What effect will Eisteddfodau have upon the extension of the English language'. It was said that the National Eisteddfod held in Cardiff in 1883 was one of the most English in its history. Before the days of the 'Rheol Gymraeg' (Welsh language only rule), many speeches from the pavilion stage would be in English. In 1938 the United States Ambassador to the United Kingdom and his son, Joseph and John F. Kennedy (the future US President), visited the National Eisteddfod in Sophia Gardens. Following the children's choir competition, Ambassador Kennedy addressed the pavilion saying that, 'It is much better teaching [our children] to sing than shoulder a rifle.' Poignant words considering how John F. Kennedy and his brother Bobby died. It was at this Eisteddfod that the campaign to win legal status for the Welsh language began in earnest and led to some rights being granted in the Welsh Courts Act 1942.

Iolo and Iago

The Globe Hotel (1731) still stands opposite the Castle Tower (having been rebuilt in 1904) and at the time of writing is a sports bar called Elevens, co-owned by the world-renowned footballer Gareth Bale. In 1773, Iolo Morganwg (his mother Ann Williams came from the prominent Mathews family of Llandaff and Radyr) accepted an invitation by Iago Twrbil of Trelai (Ely), alias James Turbervill, to meet Cylch Beirdd Caerdydd (Cardiff's bardic circle) in the Globe Hotel. Around this time Iolo refers to Welsh manuscripts in the possession of Joseph Jones, the Nailer of Cardiff who was the son of Harri Sion, the hymn writer from Pontypool. William Cobb, a yeoman and freeman of Cardiff, is also mentioned in 1782 as a collector of Welsh manuscripts. Between 1783 and 1785 Iolo lived at various locations in the Cardiff area; firstly in a house in St Mary Street, afterwards in Llandaff, and then on a 28-acre farm in Rumney, on Morfa Gwynllwg near its boundary with Peterstone Gwynllwg, inherited from his wife's uncle. He also resided for a year at Cardiff Gaol from 6 August 1786, as a result of his debts. It is said that his long-suffering wife, Peggy, conceived Iolo's only son, Taliesin, during a visit there.

In Professor Geraint Jenkins' book, *The Correspondence of Iolo Morganwg*, it is noted that Iolo's relationship with the Cardiff gaoler Thomas Morgan, a fellow Welsh speaker, was poor. Whilst in Cardiff gaol, Iolo wrote the following ballad:

> Come read my new Ballad and here you shall find
> A list of poor Debtors in Cardiff confined,
> Convicted of poverty, what a vile thing,
> And doom'd by their creditors shortly to swing.
>
> Ned Williams a mason, whose case is not rare,
> Stands indicted for build[ing] huge Castles in air…

Iolo did indeed enjoy 'building huge castles in air' and was a man of vivid imagination. He claimed that he had seen a poem in an ancient Welsh manuscript written by Robert, Duke of Normandy. He also claimed that the duke, whilst imprisoned at Cardiff Castle, learnt Welsh. Charlotte Guest, who was the first modern publisher of the Mabinogion, later translated the poem.

Iago Twrbil of Ely, who first invited Iolo to meet Cardiff's bards, was a great composer of *tribannau* (four-line poems), which at times were quite impromptu, conveying a satirical response perhaps to a fellow bard or anyone whose actions provoked a rejoinder. Whilst ploughing on Ely Farm in a field adjoining the Cowbridge Road, one of a group of girls gossiping at a well threw a clod of earth at Iago at which he broke into an instant triban:

> *Mae merched glân yn Dwllgo'd*
> *ac yn Llandaf rhai hynod.*
> *ac yn y Caerau ambell rai,*
> *ond yn Drelai cleciod.*

(There are fair maidens in Fairwater, and notable ones in Llandaff, and many a one at Caerau, but only cleckers in Ely.)

In 1751, in a letter forged by Iolo purporting to have been written by Rhys Morgan, the poet from Pengraig-nedd, to Lewis Hopkin (1708–71), another poet from Glamorgan, Iolo, through Rhys, expresses his opinion on the Welshness of the county. In reference to Cardiff, Newport, Cowbridge and Llantwit Major, he writes, 'that the common people there are now using more Welsh than English'. By all means, not all Iolo's statements were forged or without purpose. Despite describing Cardiff as 'obscure and inconsiderable', he was able to see the potential of Cardiff. In 1778 he described the location of the town 'as being the most commodious for trade than anywhere else in the principality'. Within eight years of Iolo taking out a lease on a piece of land on the side of the Taff, close to the eastern end of Cardiff bridge, an Act of Parliament was passed permitting a canal to run from Merthyr to Cardiff, a distance of 24½ miles. Iolo was certainly a man of vision, despite (or maybe because of) his eccentricity.

Welsh language in the dock

It is likely that more Welsh than English was heard in the courts, given that the majority of the people of Wales between the 16th and 18th centuries spoke only Welsh. However, the court records were kept only in English in line with the orders of the Acts of Union. Therefore, there is little in the minutes of the courts to enlighten us as to the extent of the usage of the Welsh language in areas such as Cardiff. Slander cases, on the other hand, were an exception to the rule of keeping only English records, as it was insisted that the original words and language of the cases be quoted in full and recorded in a language understood by witnesses, complainants and defendants alike. They are a very useful source of evidence.

In Wales, this exceptional practice stemmed from the case

of Gruffydd Adams against John Jenkyn Gwyn (Pembrokeshire Court of Great Sessions, 1558) where the defendant, Gruffydd, pleaded that as he was a Welshman by birth and home and, being unable to speak English, it would not have been possible for him to say the slanderous English words that were quoted in the declaration. The case did not go to trial. It is likely that the decision to accept declarations using slander in Welsh were made in the wake of a number of acts in the central courts of Westminster, where it had been adjudged that slander in a foreign language 'was not open to law' when the language used was not understandable to the witnesses or the defendants.

One of the earliest Welsh-language slander cases came from Splott in the parish of Roath in 1597 when John William said these slanderous words to William Bawdripe Esq. against Sion Willyam, a widower dwelling in Splott: *'Sion Willyam ych gwas a ddygws bwn och yd chwi och skybor a ddygws ych gwas Sion Willyam lestriad a hanner och gwenith chwi och skybor ag ei siotws ef i dŷ Sion Davidd.'* In English: 'Sion Willyam, your servant stole a bundle of your wheat from your barn and Sion Willyham, your servant, stole a bushel and a half of your wheat from your barn and shot it into Sion Dafydd's house.'

Public houses of the 18th century were often the focal point of slander cases and these provide us with opportunities to get a closer look at life in the town and surrounding parishes, as well as the extent of the usage of Welsh and English.

Cardiff and Llandaff, with their regular markets and fairs, attracted many people from other parishes. As a result, their share of slander cases was much greater than their share of the population. The fairs and markets often led to a lot of drinking and drunkenness and it would seem that the flow of slanderous words were commensurate with the flow of the beer and wine. The content of the slander was often obscene but, had it not been recorded in Welsh, the considerable amount of evidence witnessing the Welshness of Cardiff and other such areas would not have been recorded either. Below are some examples of slander cases within the town.

In 1734/5, the Five Bells in Broad Street was the centre of slanderous remarks against Ann, wife of Thomas Watkin, made by Catherine, wife of Evan Watkin the innkeeper. The words are in Welsh, and read: *'yr whore boeth, y whore gommin, y butain gomin losgedig oedd yn rhedeg ar gefnau'r gŵyr a gweision yn y Casbach.'* Giving evidence were William Walters from Cardiff, a 55-year-old labourer, and Mary Thomas, a 19-year-old spinster from Cardiff. On translation to English the slander reads, 'the hot whore, the common whore, the common burnt prostitute who ran on the backs of men and servants in Castleton.'

In 1746, Mary Harry, a spinster of Cardiff, was slandered by Mary Carey, otherwise Kerrick, the wife of Rowland Kerrick, the innkeeper of The George Inn, near the West Gate. The witnesses were Mary Jones, wife of blacksmith William Jones of Cardiff, 22-year-old cordwainer Samuel Hopkins from Cardiff, 23-year-old spinster Sara Williams from Cardiff, and 65-year-old Bridgett Prichard of St Mary's parish. The slanderous words were understood by all present: *'Yr whore, Yr whore butain wyt ti.'* In English: 'the whore, the prostitute of a whore you are.'

In 1770/1 Mary, the wife of Thomas Lewis, son of Jacob y Twr (Jacob of the Tower), brought a case against Ann, wife of William Evan of St John's parish. The witnesses were 30-year-old labourer John Owen, 27-year-old malster Charles Charles, and 39-year-old Margaret Howell – all from Cardiff. The slanderous words were: *'Ni fu neb gennyf yn erbyn y baril neu'r sistern, ac ni rhoes swllt i neb am gadw yn gownsel i. Pwy wnaeth hynny? Merch Jacob y Twr.'* In English the slanderous remarks made by Ann were: 'I didn't have anyone against the barrel or the cistern, and I didn't give a shilling to anyone to keep my counsel. Who did that? Jacob of the Tower's daughter did.'

In 1813, Cecelia Roberts brought a case against William

Prichard, both of Womanby Street, stating that he slandered her in Womanby Street outside an unnamed public house. The witnesses were 40-year-old licensee Evan Williams and 36-year-old tanner (treating leather) Thomas John, both of Cardiff. The slander was: 'Cer adre yr whore, casgliad o buteiniaid a chnafon.' In English: 'Go home you whore, a parcel of prostitutes and rogues.'

During the period 1834–40, John Howell, the late 19th-century commentator, described Cardiff as 'a place abandoned to gossip and much given to slander and scandal'. Judging from court records, such cases were at their peak in the late 18th century and were less common during the early decades of the following century. Slander cases were brought before Church Courts, Courts of the Great Session, and the Courts of the Quarter Sessions.

The records of the Church Courts of the Bishop of Llandaff are a very useful source for the study of slander cases. From the list of those slander cases within the town and the 13 surrounding parishes that I have compiled, the cases can be categorised into four groups as follows:

1) 59% of the slander cases in town were in English
2) 41% of the slander cases in town were in Welsh
3) 89% of the slander cases in the parishes were in Welsh
4) 11% of the slander cases in the parishes were in English

The total number of cases of the four categories was 111 Welsh (66%) and 58 English (34%).

Town and parish slander cases, 1710–1825

Slander cases were very common in the town and amongst the parishes of Llandaff, Llanedeyrn, St Fagans, Roath and Whitchurch. Although this study has sought to confine cases within the town and the surrounding parishes, frequently one or other of those involved in such incidents came from a parish outside the defined boundary of the study. The following areas were most likely to attract slanderous words and bad behaviour: Caerau, Canton, Crocerton, Ely, Fairwater, Leckwith, Lisvane, Llanishen, Michaelston-super-Ely, Pentyrch, Rumney, St Mellons and Y Garth. It was not uncommon for the inhabitants of Aberdare, Cowbridge, Newport or Merthyr to find themselves at the centre of a slanderous exchange in Cardiff or Llandaff, especially on market days and during either of the two annual fairs.

It is remarkable that very few inhabitants of Splott (part of Roath) were involved in Welsh slander cases. Indeed, the immediate proximity of the town to Splott, Lancros, Crockerton, Rumney, Canton and Leckwith ensured that the Welsh language enveloped the outskirts of the town from Penarth through Leckwith to Canton, Roath and Rumney. The 78 Cardiff town slander cases were divided thus: Welsh cases 41% and English cases 59%. Only Welsh speakers could be involved in Welsh slander cases, but bilingual Welsh persons could be involved in either English or Welsh cases. For example, William Gibbon from the town was involved in a Welsh slander case, whilst his unmarried sisters, Ann and Barbara, were separately entailed in English slander cases. John Sweet, a Cardiff innkeeper, and Mary Sweet were the defendants in two independent English slander cases (1718 and 1725 respectively), whilst Sherrah Sweet of Lancros on the nearby boundary of Roath and the walled town was the defendant in a 1719 Welsh slander case. Slander cases in English frequently featured participants with surnames suggesting English and Welsh opponents. For example, Hannah Meredith v Margaret Mashman (1721), Rachell Ffulks v John Griffiths (1722), Henry Watts v Thomas Lewis (1722), Margaret Williams v Richard Leigh (1724), Florence Brewer v William Evan (1730/1), Mary David v William Brewer (1734), Ann Baden, Ann Glascott and Jane Newell v Mary Lewis (1737/8), Mary Fisher v Richard John (1739), Rachel Lambert v Craddock Glascott (1739), Mary Savage v Thomas Jones

(1745), Jane Hussy v Phillip Howel (1752/53), Sarah O'Bryen v Ann Hopkins (1758), Elizabeth Thomas v Elizabeth Brewer (1771), Ann Evan v William Stone (1785), Elizabeth Williams v John Tibbott (1798), Mary Brewer v Charles Jones (1802) and Mary Lewis v John South (1817/8). These 17 examples of slander cases between Welsh and English opponents appear together with five others where the participants on both sides have English surnames. Clearly, a monoglot English speaker could not be a witness in a Welsh slander case and, likewise, a monoglot Welsh speaker could not bare witness in an English slander case. Bilingual witnesses could testify in both types of slander case as they had the linguistic skills to participate in either.

The graphs below show the percentage of the use of the Welsh language in slander cases in the town and the surrounding parishes between 1700 and 1819.

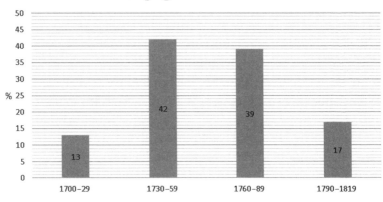

% of Welsh-language slander cases in the town

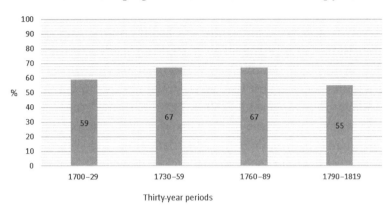

% of Welsh-language cases in Cardiff and surrounding parishes

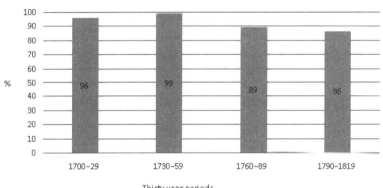

% of Welsh-language slander cases in surrounding parishes

Estimating the percentage of Welsh speakers in the town

The records of slander cases within the town present a unique opportunity to assess the percentage of people in the town who could speak Welsh during the 18th century. With the surrounding parishes of Cardiff being so Welsh, and so close to the town, it was inevitable that a considerable proportion of the population of the town would be able to speak Welsh.

Furthermore, the population living to the north of the Vale of Glamorgan and the Valleys were at that time likely to be more or less monoglot Welsh speakers. In addition, there was considerable migration from west Wales during this period, largely from Carmarthenshire to Cardiff and the surrounding area. By the early 18th century, it would be reasonable to assume that there was a monolingual Welsh presence in Cardiff, which gradually became absorbed in the town's bilingual majority. It is likely that the period 1750 to 1850, with the growth of the iron trade, the arrival of the Glamorganshire Canal and the opening of the first dock in 1839, marked the high point of the Welsh language in the town.

Counterbalancing the growth of Welsh in the town however was the critical mass of Bristol, trading on both sides of the Severn, and connected with Cardiff's Anglicised local ruling class. The division of slander cases in the town into 41% Welsh and 59% English discloses a continuum, with monoglot Welsh at one end and monoglot English at the other, with the majority bilingual Welsh with their varying degrees of fluency in the middle.

CHAPTER 4

A Town of Two Tongues

THIS CHAPTER GIVES examples from the 16th century to the 18th century of bilingualism in Cardiff. It is quite likely at this period that bilingualism was not uncommon in the town – again bearing in mind the predominance of Welsh in most of the surrounding parishes. It must be remembered, as is mentioned earlier, that the Welsh-speaking Herbert family, as the barons of Cardiff, wielded considerable influence within the town and indeed much further afield.

On a visit to Cardiff around 1537, John Leland, described as the father of English local history, records the names of the town gates in Welsh – 'Porth Crocerton', 'Porth Meisgin' (as it leads into the lordship of Miskin), 'Porth Dŵr', 'Porth Llongau' and 'Porth Senghennydd', and likewise notes 'Plas Newydd' for a newly-built mansion. Thomas Jones, the historian, expresses uncertainty for some of the names recorded, but the fact that he recorded them at all suggests strongly that Welsh was no longer a strange language within the town walls of Cardiff in the early 16th century. Later on, in 1666, in keeping with Leland's approach, we see the description 'Crocerton Gate' used in place of the East Gate. Rhys Meurig, the antiquarian, used the corresponding English names for two of the gates, 'Miskin Gate' and 'Senghennydd Gate' and also mistranslated 'Plas Newydd' to 'New Place'. In the same way Meurig describes the Castle Keep as 'Iestyn's Tower' rather than 'Tŵr Iestyn'. On the other hand he refers to 'Cwchmoel', the Welsh name for the town gaol, instead of using 'Cockmarel', the Anglo-Norman version. Likewise, he refers to rooms in the castle as *'y stafell oged'* (the harrow room) and *'y stafell wen'* (the white room) and then reverts to English when mentioning 'the black tower'.

Another early example of a bilingualist in Cardiff is the Puritan Christopher Love (1618–51). He was a native of Cardiff and acted as a chaplain to Colonel John Venn's regiment in the civil wars before becoming a fervent preacher in several churches in London. He was accused in May 1651 of organising correspondence with the exiled Charles Stuart. He was executed on Tower Hill in London for treason against the Commonwealth. When awaiting his execution he was visited by a fellow Welshman, Arise Evans (ap Rice Evans), and they baffled the English gaoler with the use of their mother tongue. Interestingly, Oliver Cromwell, the Lord Protector at the time, was the great-great-grandson of Morgan ap William, a brewer from Llanishen.[11] Nearly a century after the execution of Christopher Love, Dafydd Morgan of Coed y Gores in Llanedeyrn was also executed for treason. He was Bonnie Prince Charlie's secretary and one of the people who urged the prince to march to London. However, the prince retreated to Scotland and Morgan left in disgust, saying he would rather hang in England than starve to death in Scotland. His prophetic words came true in 1746 when he was hanged, drawn and quartered on Kennington Oval.

To return to early examples of bilingualists, we go just a little beyond the town's boundaries to the manor of Splott in the parish of Roath. In 1597, as mentioned earlier, William Bawdripe Esq. was a witness in a slander case concerning the alleged theft of wheat from his barn. The slanderous words which he testified against were uttered in Welsh. Bawdripe's family originated in Somerset and initially settled in Penmark near Rhoose. The family learnt Welsh and he was a fluent Welsh speaker and a patron of Welsh poets. Also from Somerset was

Barbara Mathew. She had learnt Welsh and was married to George Mathew of Radyr. The local poet and singer, Dafydd Benwyn, performed in nearby Rhydlafar, but also in Splott to William Bawdripe. After his death Dafydd Benwyn wrote: '*Du yw'r Ysblot dros y blaid,/ Diweniaith, da i weiniaid*' (Splott is black for his people,/ Without flattery [he was] good to the weak). Local poets such as Meurig Dafydd from Llanishen and Tomas Lewis from Llandaff flourished at that time. It is not known whether the Cardiff gaoler at the time spoke Welsh but Dafydd Benwyn called upon him to listen to a Welsh verse, asking that his nephew Ieuan ap Siencyn ab Ieuan ap Madog be released from gaol:

> *Cwnnu'i ben, canu beunydd* (Raising his head, singing daily)
> *Cwndidau yn bynnau y bydd* (Carols in bundles will be)

Roath was the first area outside the town walls to be thoroughly colonised by the Normans around 1100. The recovery of the Welsh language seems to have taken place sometime in the mid 16th century. The aforementioned slander case involving William Bawdripe in 1597 suggests that the Welsh language had returned to Roath at least around 1550. The increase of Welsh surnames in the area, as is shown in chapter two, is supported by a movement of people from the uplands.

Further evidence of the use of the Welsh language in Roath comes from a letter in 1640 sent by William Gamage of Llanedeyrn to William Herbert of Cogan Pil, stating that the people of Roath were calling on the Church to appoint a vicar who could preach in Welsh. Gamage urged Herbert to learn the language, and in the same letter he refers to the support of the families of Lewis y Fan and Kemeys Cefn Mably for the Welsh language. In the will of Edward Gamage of Roath (1730/1), a kinsman of William Gamage, are his cows with Welsh names, Cefnwen, Rossi, Pengron, Ceirios, Twbi, Tali and Gwine.

Furthermore, in 1688, the Archbishop of Canterbury was

petitioned by a list of gentry headed by one William Herbert representing 700 communicants, parishioners of Llandaff and Whitchurch of whom not one in ten understood English. It said:

> The Bishop has set over us one Mr Thomas Andrews a mere stranger to the Welsh tongue, Vicar of Roath, Vicar of St Mary's and of St John's in Cardiff, the chiefest [sic] town in the county, and farmer of the mills belonging to the said town, in the management whereof, he has been engaged for the last two years to the great danger and discomfort of our souls. May it therefore please your grace... we may be furnished with such a vicar as may be the blessing of God upon his ministry secure us from being led away...

John Jones, the scribe of Gellilyfdi in Flintshire, visited Cardiff in 1612 and listed a piece of Welsh literature, without giving it a name, in the ownership of Lambrook Stradling, of Roath, one of the grandchildren of politician and antiquary Sir Edward Stradling. Even though the 17th century was not a good time for bards and Welsh literature, there were a number of gentlemen in south-east Glamorgan who were enthusiastic Welshmen.

Rhys Meurig declared at this time that the influence of the English was dwindling in most parts of Glamorgan but that their presence was still to be seen and heard near the coast. Yet even in the cathedral parish of Llandaff, whilst William Evans was chancellor from 1550 until 1590 and Siôn ab Ieuan was the treasurer, the homes of the dignitaries of the church of Llandaff were the most important centres of literary life in Glamorgan.

John Bird (1761–1840) was born in Cardiff and, in a book which he himself published in 1796, he describes himself as a printer and bookseller, clerk to the Marquess of Bute and agent to the Phoenix Fire Office. Furthermore, he assisted the new steward, Edward Priest Richards, at manorial courts and travelled with him on rent collections, acting not only as his adviser but also – because he had learnt Welsh – as his interpreter as proceedings were quite frequently conducted in Welsh.

During encroachments on common land by the Marquess of Bute and others, there were often disputes between squatters and landowners. Bird describes one such confrontation on Cardiff heath in the summer of 1798. He records that he'd spent the morning selecting the 12 persons most suitable to be ejected from their squat. The proceedings dragged on for almost a year and it was June 1799 before a small group of officials led by John Wood Snr and John Williams of Cardiff, the deputy sheriff, accompanied by John Bird, rode towards the heath to take down the 12 illegal enclosures. They met with such barbaric resistance that Bird was sent to Cardiff to summon the volunteer cavalry. Even after the ringleaders had been taken into custody, Bird once again was sent to enlist Caerphilly Volunteers. Hastening back, he saw clouds of smoke and realised that the squat was on fire. Bird recorded that the women had fought like 'Amazonians' with pitchforks and other weapons. The squatters had claimed rights under old Welsh custom which would have allowed them to stay in their 'home' if they had built it between dawn and dusk and had smoke coming from the chimney at daybreak. The custom referring to *Tŷ Unnos* (meaning one-night house) was recognised for centuries as a legitimate act. Today the site of the confrontation can be identified by two milestones situated side by side in front of the Lidl supermarket on the corner of Maes-y-Coed Road and Caerphilly Road.

In 1838, when appointing a clerk to the markets, the town council decided that the clerk would have to be able to speak Welsh and English. The Council Minutes of 7 May 1838 record: 'Ordered that a Clerk and Inspector of Markets be appointed at a salary of £13 p.a. and that the person so appointed understands the Welsh and English languages and that notice be given of such an appointment.' A man called David Gregory was later given the post. As shown in the following advertisements in the *Cardiff and Merthyr Guardian*, the Welsh language was an advantage to those applying for a job in a shop or a business in Cardiff, even in 1849.

> To Drapers' Assistants: Wanted, a steady active young man, who understands every department of the Business practically, not under 25 years of age. One that can speak the Welsh language would be preferred. Apply to T. Miles, Draper, Cardiff.
>
> Wanted. A respectable youth, as an apprentice to the tea and grocery business. One who speaks the Welsh language would be preferred. Apply to Richd. Caldicott, 15 Duke Street, Cardiff.

As an aside, even much later the ability to speak Welsh was seen as a positive to working in the retail industry. In 1891, two-thirds of the staff of the department store David Morgan were Welsh speakers, as were over half of the staff of James Howells. In an advert in the programme of the Cardiff National Eisteddfod in 1938, Morgan Davies' Bon Marche said they had stores in every part of Cardiff and they all had Welsh-speaking staff. Morgan Davies was a benefactor of all things Welsh in Cardiff and his granddaughter was one of the first pupils of Welsh-medium education in Cardiff.

Evidently, the Welsh language was prevalent on the streets, in the shops and markets of Cardiff during the 1830s and '40s. In August 1831 when Dic Penderyn, the first working-class martyr in Wales, said his final words, '*O Arglwydd dyma gamwedd*', which mean 'Oh Lord, here is iniquity', from the gallows on St Mary Street, many in the crowd would have certainly understood the significance of his words. Penderyn was tried and found guilty following the evidence of hairdresser James Abbott and tailor William Williams. Eleven thousand people signed a petition drawn up for his reprieve but he was sentenced to death on 31 July 1831 and was publically executed two weeks later outside Cardiff's town gaol at 8 p.m.

on Saturday, 13 August. A commemorative plaque can be found on St Mary Street near the entrance to Cardiff Central Market.

The second, third and fourth Marquesses of Bute were supporters and patrons of the Welsh language. The second marquess gave the largest donation to the 1834 Cardiff National Eisteddfod and, from the stage of the Eisteddfod's pavilion, described the importance of the Welsh language as, 'the great storehouse of the people's long treasured recollections and the distinctive barrier of their nationality'. He gave free copies of the Tory Anglican monthly *Yr Haul*, which means 'the sun', to his tenants and also considered launching his own Welsh-language magazine. But there were limits to his support. When it was suggested that he showed some indulgence to a tenant who happened to be a bard, he made it clear that, 'this is not a ground to be recognised in the management of an estate'.

The second marquess had also appointed a prominent member of staff who was opposed to the Welsh language. When the reformed borough came into operation in 1836, Edward Priest Richards was appointed Town Clerk and secured a salary of £50 a year. In addition, the Council permitted him to continue his work as a solicitor in a private capacity. As agent to the second Marquess of Bute, Richards was very much the marquess' man on the Council. Bute was very concerned with the growth of Nonconformity at the expense of the Established Church whilst, at the same time, paradoxically, he was very supportive of the Welsh language which was the main language of the dissenters. Although Nonconformists were in a majority in the town and parishes, many of them would be disenfranchised and could not take control of the Council as had happened is some towns in England. Richards was convinced that Nonconformists used the Welsh language to conspire with each other and warned the marquess against supporting Welsh periodicals that promoted radical, Nonconformist and Chartist ideals. He believed that 'the continuance of the language is of no benefit to the country and... is kept up... to keep dissenters together'. Rather than supporting a Welsh periodical, he felt that it would be better to support the Society for the Promotion of Christian Knowledge (SPCK), but he knew of no one in the county who could take up the work. When he was advised to suggest Taliesin Williams, the son of Iolo Morganwg, he rejected him as being a staunch reformer who would not likely give the Establishment any cordial assistance.

In 1835, John Gove of Swansea addressed the burgesses of Cardiff for half an hour praising the qualifications of Lord James (Bute's brother) as a parliamentary candidate and, touching upon the Catholic Question, did this without creating any disturbance. It was said that this would probably not have been the case if he had spoken in Welsh, and if his comments on the Catholic Question had been fully understood by the burgesses.

The marquess' properties stretched well into the hinterland of Glamorgan, and without John Bird's assistance with the Welsh language Richards' work as an agent would have been unmanageable. During Richards' lifetime he held the positions of the Treasurer and Town Clerk to the reformed borough, as well as being agent to the second Marquess of Bute from 1824 to 1848 and to the third marquess from 1848 to 1867.

Even though the majority of references to the language in the area during the 18th century and early 19th century confirm that it was gaining ground, not everyone, such as Edward Priest Richards, welcomed that. Another example was the Honourable John Byng, a Royal Navy admiral. He went on a tour throughout Wales in 1787, creating a very negative and paradoxical picture of the condition of the language. In Newport, he said, 'We now hear as much Welsh spoken as English', and on the way into Cardiff he said, 'In our ride, I asked questions of several people who did not understand English'. Yet in Llandaff, he referred to 'the Welsh Chapel in the Cathedral', saying, 'such is the decline of that language – soon to expire like Cornish – that, whereas, there are now only seven or eight people in the Welsh congregation'. The lack of people in the congregation is not surprising as not a single Welshman was appointed as the bishop in Llandaff between 1679 and 1882. Many of those bishops might have had similar prejudicial views to those of Edward Copleston, the bishop between 1827 and 1849. In 1842 he said, 'in those areas where the Welsh language is dying it should be allowed to die out', and again in 1843 he said of the language to the Dean of Llandaff, William Bruce Knight, 'I wonder they are not tired of this barren nonsense'. The Cardiff parishes of St John and St Mary were under the patronage of the Dean and Chapter of Gloucester Cathedral and these livings were used to finance young clerics in Gloucester. The living of St John's was for John Webb, an absentee cleric between 1821 and 1864, and those who stood in for him held services in English. It was said of Webb's period, '... the leadership of the parish was missing, and the result was that the parish stagnated for well over forty years'.

As Byng continued his journey through Llandaff he referred to the harpist as one 'who rattled away to my amusement in Welsh with Mr Traherne'. Then again, this time in Cardiff, at the Cardiff Arms, the subject of discussion was Welsh – the language that he was so certain would die like Cornish but seemed to be unable to avoid talking about it. The 'Honourable' John Byng eventually reveals his prejudice against the Welsh, without any hesitation, shame or respect for his hosts by declaring, 'To me the Welsh appeared as inferior to the common English in ability as they are in stature and comeliness; particularly the women, who are very ugly and dwarfish'.

Had Edward Priest Richards been a contemporary of Byng's, and also been present at the Cardiff Arms at the time of Byng's rant, it is questionable whether he would have drawn a line between the naked ignorance of the dishonourable Byng and his own misgivings concerning the Welsh language. A few years following his visit to Wales, Byng was executed for his failure to regain the island of Menorca from the French.

Jottings from the 18th century

There are two 18th-century diaries that give us greater detail about life in the town and surrounding parishes. Indirectly, through the use of nicknames and place-names, many of the entries provide an insight into the use of the Welsh language in the area at that time. They are the diaries of Thomas Morgan and William Thomas.

Thomas Morgan's diary, 1708–36

Thomas Morgan meticulously recorded daily details of income and expenditure in his notebook, often referring to individuals by their nicknames. He frequently rode on horseback into Cardiff to transact his business and would call at the Red House, sometimes called 'Y Tŷ Coch', or the Angel for a friendly drink. Indeed, he mentions visits to no fewer than 13 public houses amongst his notes. Before retiring each night, he recorded details of his income and expenditure for the day. As both a farmer and a lawyer, he had a modest income. Though it is not certain exactly where he lived, his movements suggest that he was living either in Rumney at Llanrhymney Hall or possibly in Llanedeyrn near Coed y Gores, the family home of his ancestors.

The main relevance and importance of his notebook, from my point of view, is the picture it paints of a Welsh community in the early 18th century. It embraces Cardiff town and much of the surrounding parishes as Thomas Morgan's dealings took him from place to place. Although the notebook is not written in Welsh, the nicknames suggest strongly that here was a wide community within which Welsh was the familiar language. For example, he mentions 'Mary Tennis Court' and 'Dic y Fuwch', who were all named after the public houses they ran. Mary

Tennis Court kept an inn of that name which today is known as the Owain Glyndŵr; and Dic y Fuwch (Dic the Cow) kept the Red Cow in Womanby Street, which was officially reopened for a period in 2009/10 as Y Fuwch Goch.

The personal names and place-names recorded amongst his notes, together with details of his transactions, bring the reader somewhat closer to the life of a middle-class gentleman in the town, who also had close relations with those living in the areas of Roath, Rumney and Llanedeyrn in particular.

His note on the purchase of a *pedwran* of malt is a reminder that Welsh measures, such as the *llestraid* (168 lbs), the *pedoran* (42 lbs) and the *pedwran* (10.5 lbs) were in use, though they were not deemed to be official in the Cardiff market until 1758 when it was made compulsory to use Welsh measures.

The process of fixing surnames in the area of Rumney and Llanedeyrn seems in many cases to have been incomplete or merely unofficially replaced by nicknames. The notebook records: John Catwg (of Llangatwg Farmhouse in Llanedeyrn), Thomas ab Evan of the 'Denas', George Vann (presumably of the family of Lewis y Fan), David Rumney, Morgan Whitehorse, Morgan of Splott and Ann Morgan Greenway as the common names used at this time by Thomas Morgan.

It is possible that the family of Lewis Hendry, cousins Lewis Pendry and Thomas Pendry, had a fixed surname based on the local farm name, Hendre, mispronounced as Hendry. Or had the family dropped the 'ap' so that eventually they all adopted either Pendre or perhaps Penry as their established surname?

Thomas Morgan's notes contain a large number of place-names such as Lewis Penmark, Thomas Glascot (formerly Glascoed), Catherine Blackwears, Howard of Roth (Roath), Morgan Lancros, Gŵr Roswg (husband of Roswg Farm, Llanedeyrn), Lewis Faindre Fach in St Mellons, Wm Lewis, Bristol Fach (tobacco shop in Pentyrch), Abraham Craig yr Haul, Williams Llangwm, Lewis Llanishen, Edward Radir, David Penyrhewl and Y Warth – the large lowland area lying between the rivers Rhymney and Severn. He records the Welsh usage for 'to go ashore' – '*i fynd i'r Warth*'.

In addition, there are also trade names such as Peggy Coyders (woodcutter), Dick Tinker, Betty Tanner, William Jones 'Copler' (Cobler – Welsh habit of hardening a letter 'b' to a 'p'), as well as nicknames such as Ann tîn bach (Ann small bottom), Bill Jonas, David Bach, and Mr Seys (someone who spoke English as well as Welsh).

Farmhouses and other place-names

The notebook is rich with names of farmhouses and other place-names: Yr Hendre, Llwyn y Grant, Penyrhewl, Tŷ Du, Tŷ Llwyd, Tir Llwyd, Coed Kernyw, Tŷ'n y Cyw (Roath), Greenway farm, the Pandy Rumney, the Old Rumney Posthouse, Maesllech, Cefn Coed – Cyncoed, Roath, Splott. These are the public houses he mentions: King's Head, The Tennis Court, Y Fuwch Goch (The Red Cow), Ceffyl Gwyn (The White Horse), Faindre Fach, Llanishen, Y Tŷ Coch (The Red House) – later replaced by the Cardiff Arms, Craig yr Haul, The Lamb, Dobbin's Pit, Cock Ale House, The Shoulder of Mutton Inn, The Angel, Rumney Inn, The Five Bells (Broad St, Cardiff), The Globe Inn (corner of Angel Street and Womanby Street) and The Unicorn in Llanedeyrn.

Thomas Morgan's frequent spelling and pronunciation of *cabach* in place of cabbage is similar to that of the Plunge Gate (1578) and the Blunch Gate (1715, 1738) in place of the original English Blount's Gate (1485) and the Blount's Yate (1542–3). This change reflects the growing influence of Welsh pronunciation at that time within the area generally. See also the change of Cyncoed to Kingot and Hengoed to Hengot.

William Thomas' diary, 1762–95

Another source of interest showing the position of the Welsh language in Cardiff and the parishes is William Thomas' diary. He was born in 1727 in Michaelston-super-Ely. Thomas was a schoolteacher in one of Griffith Jones' Welsh circulatory schools. In these schools a quarter of a million people, almost half the population of Wales, became literate in the native tongue during the period 1731 to 1777. Even though William Thomas was a Welsh teacher, he didn't keep his diary in Welsh but frequently refers to places using their Welsh names, e.g. Monydd Bychan (rather than Mynydd Bychan) for the Great Heath and Y Waun Ddyfal for the Little Heath. His sentences seem to be based partially on Welsh syntax. For example, 'He left all to his brother John Deere an old clergyman who was out on sea with Sir Cloudy [*sic*] Shovel, deceased, but now these many years past he lived, he unmarried, with his brother in Penlline.'

He often spelt place-names as they were colloquially pronounced, e.g. Eglwys Shilan in place of Eglwys Ilan. Likewise, he repeatedly wrote Rafe for Roath, Ton Dwylis for Tongwynlais, The Wenny for Ewenni and Pendwlan for Pendoylan.

William Thomas manages somehow to have notes for each day, referring to births, deaths, thefts, murders, marriages, militia men absconding, riots in Bristol between militia men and butchers, men leaving their women, wives leaving their husbands, local people dying in the West Indies from drinking too much rum, gentry confiscating cattle in lieu of rents unpaid, and cock-fights at a local inn called Twlc yr Huwch (The Pigsty).

He refers to the migration cycle whereby the Welsh moved from Carmarthenshire to the Cardiff area and then on to Bristol where the Bristolians had almost all gone abroad: 'Welshmen these last few years have almost fill [*sic*] Bristol, that often two Welshmen can be found to one Englishman, for the English goes [*sic*] abroad and Welshmen fill England in their stead.'

Bristol was then second only to London in size and importance and contained large numbers of Welsh exiles. The diary also uncovers a considerable amount of migration within

Wales, more especially of Carmarthenshire people who had come to live and work in Cardiff or the Vale. During the year 1766, the diarist refers in passing to nine such people from Carmarthenshire, three from Pembrokeshire, and one each from Brecknockshire and Anglesey. On the other hand, in the same year, he refers only twice to 'an Englishman by birth' and once to 'a Cornish gentleman'.

His diary reveals that people at this time were moving not merely from town to town, or even from one county to the next, but from Bristol they would go to the West Indies or other parts of America. His diary notes in 1769 the death of two young Welsh-speaking brothers from Michaelston-super-Ely who had joined the slave trade to the West Indies.

Thomas was sympathetic to the needs of the poor people. In his entry on 4 January 1767, he criticised George Withers of Cwrt-yr-Ala, the overseer of the woods at Wrinston belonging to the Ffonmon Estate, for his eagerness to have offenders, both male and female, whipped in the churchyards for cutting wood. The diarist, however, seems to have needed sympathy when he recorded on 14 May 1779 that a John Rees had married his aunt and godmother, Nancy Thomas of Cog, at Meiryn (Marshfield). She was Rees' elder by 20 years and, moreover, a woman that Thomas himself had his heart set upon, as he declared, 'This was she I was deceived by a Trick she was to be my wife. How vain is man?'

His daily entries again and again are coloured by the use of nicknames. For example, 26-year-old Moll Goch (redhaired Moll), born in Llantwit Major, who died on 15 December 1763. She is described as a common whore and was found dead in a ditch near St Mellons. According to Thomas, 'She was a short woman, very ready in Welsh or English, not a beauty and kept herself very slovenish. Her mother is married to a second husband and lives in Cardiff.' He also mentions a second Moll who is nicknamed Mol Annifyr, meaning Moll the unpleasant in English. He also mentions David Goyder (David woodcutter), John y Cwrw (John the beer), John y Defaid (John the warts), and George Dew (Fat George). The list goes on, and one wonders how all those who had had such names bestowed upon them felt. On 24 December 1763 he refers to John Plummer, who found in a ditch the skeleton of John y Sais (John the Englishman), probably so-called because of his background rather than his ability to speak both Welsh and English.

On 7 October 1791 he records the execution of 'Henry James of 25 years age, from Eglwys Ilan by birth, and Catherine Griffith (Catty Goch) of 31 years of age, from Llanillturn, for breaking into the house of Mrs Price of Park in Llanillturn'. The execution took place 'at Waun Ddyfal' (where Hewl Plwca, now City Road, and Merthyr Road, now Albany Road, then met and is still referred to as death junction by Cardiffians).

He further referred to another skeleton found by 'Edward y Galchwr' (Edward lime-burner) and family in the Parson's House in St Andrews: 'His bones were found in the partition in the Hall.' Altogether, the skeletons of four Scotsmen were found, whom it is believed were murdered whilst travelling in the area selling their goods.

On 30 September 1762, he recorded the death of:

William John of Canton, lately of the Grange looking after the sheep, has drowned after the night of the Cardiff Fair, the 29th instant. He was 60 years of age and married with a second wife who was with him this day, and both drunk, for he had that morning about 52 shillings from John Jenkin of Canton; all his gains from the last harvest. But some do report that run away he did, being his wife giving herself to whoring and drinking and was the night of the fair an open drunk and a publick [sic] whore thro the town. She is from Carmarthenshire by birth. Her husband is called Will Drydy Will, meaning Will the third Will, as his mother had three base sons all named Will of whom he was the third.

85

In March 1766 he records the death of a relation to Iolo Morganwg:

On the 29th of March 1766, was buried in Peterstone Wentllwg, William Robert, son of the late Thomas of the Corner House of the Cross in St. Andrews, deceased. He died very wealthy. He that broke his leg about this sixteen months past, and then report came of his death. William Robert was uncle to the wife of Iolo Morganwg. She inherited Pen-y-Pil in Rumney after his death.

The death of two of Iolo's fellow literati was also noted in the diary. Firstly Joseph Jones, who collected Welsh manuscripts and was made a burgess of Cardiff in 1767: 'Was buried in Cardiff since the 30th of June last (1784) Jo. Jones the Nailer of 55 years of age, from a lingering disease; father of many children, an Anabaptist, and somewhat of a poet.' Secondly William Cobb, who is noted in the Cardiff records as having been made both a freeman and a burgess of the Cardiff Borough in 1782: 'This four weeks or more past was buried in Cardiff, William Cobb, a good lawyer's clerk of about 50 years of age.'

Another interesting entry in the diary is that of the death in London of Dr Richard Price (1723–91), who was a philosopher, politician and statistician. He was the son of the Rev. Rhys Price of Tŷ'n y Ton, Bridgend. Richard Price was the author of *Observations on the Nature of Civil Liberty*. Although he never set foot in America, he was a great advocate of American Independence and his ideological contributions were greeted warmly there. In his absence he was awarded an honorary degree from the University of Yale in 1781, along with George Washington.

A more ephemeral link is that Price was a cousin of Ann Maddocks (née Thomas), the maid of Cefn Ydfa, and supposedly the inspiration of the love song, *Bugeilio'r Gwenith Gwyn* (Gathering the White Wheat). Folklore has it that Ann was in love with Wil Hopcyn (1700–41), an artisan and poet. When she married, however, it was to Anthony Maddocks.

In an age when the pressures of Calvinistic Methodism were beginning to take root, they didn't seem at first to have had much of a restraining influence on the general population. The diarist notes frequently events, such as this on 9 January 1792: 'The death near Abergaveny of William John the Harper, called William Bach y Telynwr from his short stature. A skilful harper of about 55 years of age, and a man by report that killed himself with drink.'

Another similar example:

> Was buried in St Fagans, John Thomas, a Tyler of 69 years of age from seven days sickness, but had been last winter sick the most of it. He was the father of four children, but not one of them came to perfection, nor to have a Christening. He was son to old James Thomas of Wenvoe, a Tyler deceased, and a very expansive man by drinking.

The diarist was a man of moderation, a lover of literature who had an aversion for celebrations when music and revelry fired by drink were taken to extremes. There were by no means a shortage of fiddlers and harpists, and we have the impression that Calvinistic Methodism had not yet suppressed the folk traditions during the lifetime of William Thomas. One could feel his joy when reporting on the young mother who had had two sets of twins and a set of triplets, all seven of whom survived. Surely a rare pleasure when contrasted with the infant mortality rate which seemed to be extremely high, whilst drunkenness and poverty were also rampant. William Thomas' diary is a rare treasure, providing a window through which we can study life in this corner of Wales and beyond during the latter half of the 18th century.

CHAPTER 5

Conforming and Non-Conforming

The Established Church

In the 19th century Thomas Phillips, a benefactor of education in Wales and the founder of Llandovery College, claimed that the Established Church had the responsibility under the Act of Uniformity 1662 to ensure Welsh services throughout the whole of Wales. But in the diocese of Llandaff, and especially in those areas that came under Anglo-Norman influence, the responsibility of the Church was to the English language. Thus, Welsh-language services were held as additions to the main services in parishes such as Roath, Llandaff and Whitchurch, although Welsh was the spoken language of these parishes in the 16th century and probably earlier in the case of the latter two. In 1640, the parishioners of Roath made an appeal for a Welsh service in opposition to an English vicar who, it appears, was not fluent in the language of the people.

Furthermore, as mentioned earlier, in 1688 there was a petition addressed to the Archbishop of Canterbury, headed by a man named William Herbert and signed by 700 communicants of whom not one in ten could speak English. Following the death of the previous bilingual vicar, David Price, in 1687, the bishop appointed a vicar who could not speak Welsh.

In 1771 in the parish of Llanilltern, near St Fagans, the local church was busily displacing the Welsh language amongst the young people. Although church services were in Welsh, the catechism for the young people was mainly in English.

Within the diocese of Llandaff from 1771 to 1850, surveys were held every three years in each parish. The questions asked included: how often are services held, in what language, what is the average attendance in the morning, how many attend the Sunday school, and how many attend the evening service.

Dr W.T.R. Pryce, a geography and social sciences academic, places the use of the Welsh language in the Established Church into five categories:

Category 1: Services in Welsh only
Category 2: Mainly Welsh
Category 3: Alternatively Welsh and English
Category 4: Mainly English – Welsh occasionally
Category 5: English only

Referring to the attitude of the Bishop of Llandaff in 1811, Pryce states: 'It was in Llandaff diocese, however, that the bishop's stated language policy seems to have been most unrealistic... bilingual Welshmen, with all their various ranges of fluency in the language, were expected to attend services held exclusively in English.' Certainly, the policy was no better in 1842 when Bishop Copleston of Llandaff suggested that in 'those areas where the Welsh language was dying it should be allowed to die out', for he added Wales was not a subordinate but an integral component part of one common country: 'we seek to be one with her in language as we have for centuries been one in religion.'

The extensive work of Pryce[12] on the bishops' surveys creates a detailed picture of the linguistic boundaries from the middle of the 18th century to the middle of the 19th century. R.M. Thomas,[13] however, questions the extent to which the language of the Established Church reflected the language of the people.

Thomas was of the opinion that clergymen in the Established Church had a tendency to displace the Welsh language not because the people had lost their command of Welsh, but because the churchmen were either lacking in their knowledge of Welsh or were frequently ready to meet the needs of the squire's family regardless of Welsh being the first language of the regular worshippers. In Thomas' linguistic survey of south Wales, he considers that the bishops' surveys overstress the Englishness of areas where Welsh Nonconformists were actually numerically predominant. According to the religious census of 1851, Nonconformists attending their places of worship outnumbered those attending the Established Church by a considerable margin.

In order to obtain a more detailed view of the local situation, evidence has been gathered from the 15 parishes that today form the component parts of Cardiff and include 11 bishops' reports dating from 1771 to 1850. At the beginning of the reports there were few Nonconformist places of worship to provide evidence affecting the linguistic boundaries as defined by the research of Dr W.T.R. Pryce. Yet, as the Nonconformist chapels grew in number, it became possible to delineate the linguistic boundaries with a greater deal of accuracy.

Interestingly, the bishops' returns showed a considerable increase in the number of churches giving preference to Welsh. In 1771, the Church reports in the Cardiff area placed the use of Welsh between Pryce's categories of two and three, whereas some 24 years later, the average category for the use of Welsh had improved and lay between categories one and two. Of the 12 churches that existed at that time, eight of them held all their services in Welsh, three were held mostly in Welsh (Pryce's category two), and St John's, as usual, made no return. By 1809, the average language return had risen slightly to category two and by 1850 the average response to the language return was 2.8, almost category three which corresponded to churches holding bilingual services. By that time, four of the churches were holding their services completely in English (category five). These were St John's, St Fagans, Roath and Llandaff. Curiously, St Mary's Church, which had recently been rebuilt, was a category four church under the leadership of their Welsh-speaking vicar, William Leigh Morgan, as Welsh services were held in a schoolroom for a reasonable portion of its members. Shortly afterwards they set up their own Welsh-language church, Yr Holl Seintiau (All Saints), located, ironically, on the corner of Tyndall Street and Ellen Street in the heart of the Irish quarter with its large Catholic population. A Welsh-language church was promised by the second Marquess of Bute and completed after his death by his widow. All Saints became an English cause in 1875, but following the appointment of the first Welsh bishop in Llandaff for over 200 years in 1883, Dewi Sant Church was opened in 1890. It still flourishes today as the only Anglican church in Wales to conduct its business entirely through the medium of Welsh.

Table: Pryce's categorisation of the Welsh language in Cardiff and surrounding parishes according to bishops' visitation reports, 1771–1851

Parish	1771	1774	1781	1784	1788	1791	1795	1809	1813	1848	1850
Caerau	2	1/2	1	1	n/n[14]	n/n	1	1	1	3	1
Llandaff	n/n	3	n/n	3	n/n	n/n	n/n	2	n/n	3	5
Llanedeyrn	3	n/n	n/n	1	1	1	1	n/n	1	1	1
Llanishen	3	2	1	3	1	1	1	2	3	n/n	2
Lisvane	1	1	n/n	1	1	1	1	n/n	1	n/n	1
Michaelston-super-Ely	2	3	3	n/n	1	1	1	n/n	n/n	1	1
Pentyrch	3	3	3	n/n	n/n	n/n	n/n	n/n	n/n	2	3
Radyr	3	3	1	2	1	1	n/n	1	1	3	1
Roath	3	3	2	n/n	3	n/n	n/n	3	3	5	5
Rumney	1	n/n	3	2	n/n	n/n	n/n	n/n	n/n	2	1
St Fagans	2	3	3	3	3	3	n/n	n/n	3	4	5

St John	5	n/n	5	5	n/n	n/n	n/n	n/n	n/n	5	5
St Mary[15]	–	–	–	–	–	–	–	–	–	4	4
St Mellons	3	3	3	n/n	n/n	n/n	n/n	n/n	2	3	2
Whitchurch	n/n	1	2	3	n/n	3	1	n/n	3	3	3

The local foundations of the different Nonconformist denominations

The Independents

In 1672 John French, a native of Cardiff and a former minister at Wenvoe, obtained a licence to hold religious services in his house under the leadership of Alderman John Archer[16], also of Cardiff. In 1696, a chapel was built in Womanby Street on a 999-year lease.

In the same year as building the chapel, the Rev. Rhys Prytherch (Rice Protheroe), a minister from Carmarthen, came to Cardiff to take up the challenge of ministering the small gathering at Womanby Street. It appears that the chapel was English from the beginning, although all the ministers who followed Protheroe were Welsh speakers up to the 1840s. During the ministry of the Rev. William James (1788–1845), services were held in both English and Welsh occasionally. William James' sermons could carry through the morning and into the afternoon. Their length and delivery did not attract a large gathering.

The Independents, no doubt finding the Rev. William James' preaching somewhat lengthy and his Welsh sermons too infrequent, founded a meeting place in a coach house in 1826. The coach house was situated in a rather stark building, appropriately named Cwrt Glandŵr, backing on to the east side of the River Taff. The leaking roof of the coach house and the frequent threat from the river acted as an incentive to acquire a minister and a place of worship located on a firm foundation. In 1827 Lewis Powell accepted the offer to become the minister of the small gathering, though he expressed his concern that the site at Crocerton, near today's St David's Centre, was too far away from the town, with only a few houses in its immediate vicinity. Nonetheless, through the minister's enthusiasm, he ensured that the money required for building a chapel was raised and Ebeneser was opened in 1828. Lewis Powell used to keep inside his hat a number of witty phrases in Welsh and ragged English, such as '*Brenin nobl yw common sense*', in English, 'common sense is the noble king'. Ebeneser was later responsible for the creation of a number of other chapels in Cardiff. These were Mount Stuart in the Docks, Severn Road in Canton, Minny Street in Cathays and Bethlehem in Splott. There was also a Bethlehem in Gwaelod-y-Garth and Bronllwyn in Pentyrch. Tairhirion in Llanilltern was founded in 1760 and Beulah in Rhiwbeina in 1812; all of which were Welsh causes.

Cardiff Wesleyans
The Cardiff Wesleyan Society was set up in 1740 and John Wesley opened a meeting place in 1743, called the New Room, situated in Church Street in town. After this, however, the first cause failed but was founded again around 1770. Welsh-speaking and English-speaking members worshipped together and though preachers, such as Harri Llwyd from Rudry and Timothy Thomas, formerly of Llanharry, preached in Welsh, services up to this time were mostly in English. Despite this, according to the Wesleyan historian David Young, in 1775 Welsh was the language of the people of Cardiff and the holding of English services was a great drawback to the growth of Welsh Calvinistic Methodism at that time. The appointment of John Hughes of Brecon to the circuit in 1795 brought new life to the cause. The English- and Welsh-speaking members met in the same building until 1829, and before this it was difficult to differentiate the history of one group from the other. The register for the two groups was started in 1796, and written on the front page was: 'in this English Registration Book, there have been registered children baptised by the Welsh minister,

Old Wesleyan Chapel, Church Street

and in the Welsh Registration Book, there have been registered children baptized by the English ministers.'

It is understood that the national Welsh Wesleyan cause began in 1805 when missionary Griffith Owen worked amongst the Welsh. He was succeeded by William Evans in 1806, and then by Griffith Hughes in 1807. By 1809, the Cardiff Welsh Wesleyan Circuit had 560 members, whilst the English Circuit had only 156 members.

The Calvinistic Methodists

In the 19th century there were in Cardiff and the surrounding parishes at least four meeting places of Calvinistic Methodists, namely in St Fagans, Llanedeyrn, Llanishen and Cardiff town. There is only the occasional mention of Calvinistic Methodists in Cardiff before this but following the split between the Calvinists and the Wesleyans, the former were propelled into building their own chapel on the banks of the canal near the tunnel behind Plymouth Street in Crocerton, today's Queen Street. In 1810 they took out a lease on this location and registered a chapel on 15 February 1812. Edward Coslett, the blacksmith and lay preacher from Casbach (Castleton), was one of the trustees. By 1827 the Calvinists had bought a new chapel, Seion, in Trinity Street where the old town library now stands. When the old chapel on the canal bank became vacant, the Welsh Wesleyans were quick to purchase the building and stayed there until they bought a chapel on the junction of Union Street and Ebeneser Street that they named Bethel.

Bethania, Butetown, known as the Dock's church, was established in 1856 and the minister had such a winning personality that he could attract some of the best preachers in Wales to his chapel. He would announce the preaching festival, thus: *'blwyddyn i heddiw bydd Dr Owen Thomas yma, a Dr David Saunders, a'r Parchedig David Charles Davies. Os digwydd na ddônt hwy, daw pregethwyr mawr eraill yn eu lle: Bethania Dock am Efengyl, cofiwch.'* In English: 'A year today Dr Owen Thomas will be here, and Dr David Saunders, and the Rev. David Charles Davies. If it happens that they don't come, other great preachers will take their place: Bethania Dock for the gospel, remember.'

St Fagans: Howel Harris visited St Fagans in 1740 and 1741, preaching on both occasions in Lewis and Christina Dafydd's house, Cribyn Cadog, and this was the beginning of the cause in St Fagans. After Christina's death in 1742, the meeting place was moved to the house of Isaac Dafydd on the banks of the River Ely. When Isaac died in 1760, the cause moved once again, this time to the house of Thomas Llywelyn of Ysgubor Fawr (The Big Barn). After the death of Thomas Llywelyn, Bartholomew Howel's house was rented by Christopher Bassett, the curate of St Fagans, and here the meetings were held until a chapel was built in 1837 as a Welsh cause.

Llanedeyrn: Two Calvinistic Methodist councillors were connected with Llanedeyrn, namely Richard Thomas and Samuel Jeremiah. In 1740, 'it was recorded that there were four members, three of whom know the Lord Jesus and the other who is under the act'. There is no further reference to this cause until a church called Pen-y-Groes was opened in 1840 as a Welsh cause, on the crossroads at Llanedeyrn, now the site of a Welsh-medium primary school which opened in September 2009 and is appropriately called Pen-y-Groes.

St Mellons: The founder of this cause in St Mellons, or Llaneirwg in Welsh, was Edward Coslett, a blacksmith who was born in Machen and moved to Casbach (Castleton). When the owner of the blacksmith's dwelling place was not willing for him to hold Nonconformist meetings in his house, Coslett had to move and he went to St Mellons. There, in 1780, he established the Calvinistic Methodist cause in the parish and named it Bethania. Coslett was followed as minister in 1801 by the famous preacher, Henry Jones Llaneirwg.

The Baptists
Even though a permanent cause was not established in the area until 1782, dwelling houses were licensed as places to worship by the Baptists as long ago as 1751/2. For example, the house of Lewis Watkins of Roath was registered as a meeting house of Baptists.

Lisvane: To the east of the area of study, a Baptist chapel was established in 1743 at Tŷ Du (Rogerstone). In Casbach (Castleton) it was claimed that 60 members were present in 1716/17, even though the year of the chapel's incorporation with the Welsh Baptists was not until 1823. In 1782, Harri Rees left Rogerstone to live in Tai Mawr, Lisvane, and from then onwards the cause of the Welsh Baptists in the parish grew. A lease for 999 years was taken out in 1794 on a patch of land known as 'Y Dderwen Deg' (the Fair Oak).

St Mellons: The first record of the Baptist cause in St Mellons is a note in the book of the chapel, stating that it was in 1794 that the Rev. John Hier of Bethesda, Rogerstone, had preached in a dwelling house. Members met in the poorhouse until a chapel was opened in 1830.

Table: Nonconformist Chapels in Cardiff and area, pre-1801

Name & location	Denomination	Established	Language Category	Worshippers, 1851
Womanby Street	Independent	1672	4	120
Church Street	Wesleyan	1770[17]	4	700
Tabernacl (St Fagans)	C.M.	1780	1	190
Bethania (St Mellons)	C.M.	1780	1	210
Derwendeg (Lisvane)	Baptist	1789	1	124
Caersalem (St Mellons)	Baptist	1794	1	150

Nonconformity, 1801–41

Bethany English-Language Baptist Church, Hewl y Cawl (Wharton Street)

According to Bethany's register, the chapel dates from 1804. It was established by a handful of people from Herefordshire, and in their midst was Thomas Hopkin, the son of Lewis Hopkin who was the minister of the Congregational church at Bromyard in Herefordshire. There seems to have been a strong link between Herefordshire and south-east Wales. Indeed, the first Welsh-language Baptist chapel was founded around 1641, but in the Olchon valley within the boundaries of Herefordshire rather than in Wales. The Welsh language was still spoken in that county up to the early 19th century. It is therefore not surprising that the opening ceremony of Bethany included two sermons in Welsh, and thereafter sermons in Welsh were a frequent occurrence. When Thomas Lewis was ordained as the first minister in 1809 it was noted that 'the Welch [*sic*] were not forgotten in the arrangements for the day'. In 1815 another Welsh preacher became the minister of the chapel, namely William Jones, a native of Llangadog in Carmarthenshire, who learned English on going to college. It was said about him: 'When he first came to Cardiff his knowledge of Welsh was of great advantage to him in his visiting, but his public ministrations were generally confined to the English tongue.' When a new chapel was opened to serve the cause in 1821, four of the eight sermons were in Welsh. William Jones died in 1855. He was a Welsh author of renown and it was not until 1857 that the chapel left the Union of Welsh Baptists when appointing an English minister, the Rev. Alfred Tilly. One would have expected Bethany to have given up its use of the Welsh language completely as soon as the Tabernacl Welsh Baptist chapel opened its doors in the town of Cardiff in 1813. On studying the Bethany register from 1804 to 1837 however, it appears that the Welsh were the majority in the chapel at that time.

Cardiff Town

Of the 18 places of worship that were established in the wider area between 1800 and 1840, all except two were Welsh in language. In the town alone, when the Welsh Wesleyans made their home in the old Calvinistic chapel on the banks of the canal, four of the eight of the town's places of worship were completely Welsh medium by 1829:

Welsh	English
Tabernacl (Baptist), The Hayes	St John's Church, Church Street
Seion (Calvinistic Methodist), Trinity Street	Womanby Street Congregational Church
Ebeneser (Independent), Crocerton	Bethany (Baptist), Wharton Street
Bethel (Wesleyan), Canal Bank	Wesleyan, Church Street

It seems likely at this time that Welsh-language churches in the town were more popular than the English causes; St John's Church was neglected and was said to be standing still. There had never been a large congregation at Womanby Street and the minister's preaching was described as 'deadly'. In Bethany, there were only 51 members in 1820 and even though the English Wesleyan church enjoyed growth after 1827, before that the Welsh Wesleyan church was growing the faster of the two. The Tabernacl had over 200 members by 1831 and a substantial number of Sunday school scholars. Seion, the Welsh Calvinistic Methodist chapel, had a fine building with places for up to 600 worshippers, and Ebeneser, the Welsh Independent chapel, was enjoying the busy and enthusiastic ministry of the Rev. Lewis Powell. It seems incredible today but when Tabernacl moved to its current site in 1821, it overlooked fields and one of the old pathways to the chapel is preserved today in the Morgan Arcade and is called Tabernacle Lane. When Ebeneser was built in 1828 at the location of what is now the St David's Shopping Centre, it was described as being out of town with only a few houses nearby.

Table: Nonconformist chapels in Cardiff and the parishes, pre-1840

Name & location	Denomination	Established	Welsh/English category	Worshippers 1851
Womanby Street	Independent	1672	4/5	120
Bethany	Baptist	1804	4/5	570
Tabernacl	Baptist	1813	1	850
Seion	C.M.	1827	1	428
Ebeneser, Crocerton	Independent	1826	1	200
Bethel	Wesleyan	1827	1	100
Church St	Wesleyan	1827	5	200
Pen-y-lan, Wh'church	Wesleyan	1800	1	130
Pen-y-Lan, Wh'church	Wesleyan	1810	5	100
Ebeneser, Wh'church	C.M.	1808	1	76
Llandaff, City of Ll'daf	Wesleyan	1839	1	50
Trelai, Llandaff	Wesleyan	1806	1	60
Gilead, Rumney	Wesleyan	1808	1	50
Bethel, Radyr	C.M.	1817	1	150
Ainon, Wh'church	Baptist	1832	1	560
Ararat, Wh'church	Baptist	1824	1	300
Capel Gwilym, Llanishen	Baptist	1831	1	30
Tai Hirion, Llanilltern	Independent	1822	1	73
Horeb, Pentyrch	C.M.	1839	1	205
Bethlehem, Gwaelod-y-Garth	Independent	1831	1	179
Penuel, Pentyrch	Baptist	1838	1	189
Pen-y-Groes, Llanedeyrn	C.M.	1840	1	41
Caersalem, St Mellons	Baptist	1830	1	200
Soar, St Mellons	Independent	1837	1	60
Bethania, St Mellons	C.M.	1820	1	170

Of the 24 Nonconformist chapels built between 1800 and 1840, 22 of them were Welsh-medium institutions. Bethany, on the corner of Wharton Street, was predominantly English medium, whilst the Wesleyan chapel in Church Street on the other hand had become completely English medium when the Welsh section of the congregation first moved to the old Calvinist Methodist chapel on the canal bank in 1827 and to a new building on the corner of Union and Ebeneser streets in 1838.

By 1845 there were 42 places of worship in the town and its surrounding parishes. Of these, 30 were predominately Welsh medium, six were bilingual and the remaining six used English only. The town had three churches: St John's built around 1400, Saint Mary's on Bute Street, built in 1843, and St David's Catholic Church built in 1842.

During the period 1845 to 1861, 23 new places of worship were established and brought the total in the area of study to 63. Of the new causes, 12 were Welsh medium and 11 were English. The setting up of 11 new English-medium churches and chapels reflected the substantial influx of people from the West Country of England. Even the small village of Ely was affected by the introduction of English services in the Wesleyan chapel to cater for English incomers such as the local stationmaster and the engineer of the water pump. Also, the Government's 'Blue Books' report on education and religion in Wales in 1847 sought to undermine both Nonconformity and the widespread use of Welsh. The Welsh were accused of general immorality, and it would seem that the growing concept of bilingualism was viewed by the English Establishment not as a widening of horizons or an enrichment of a culture, but as the effrontery of a small nation to be different from its unsympathetic neighbour. However, the opening of English-language chapels could have strengthened the Welsh language in the Welsh chapels. In 1859, one Sunday school in Tabernacl, The Hayes, changed from English to Welsh medium and in 1863 it was

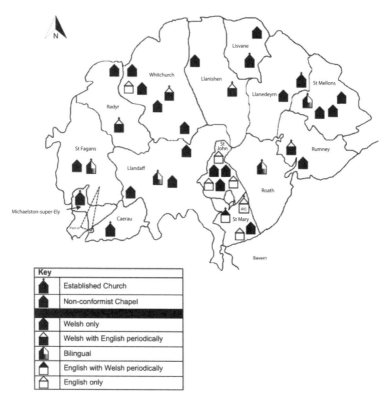

The language of places of worship in Cardiff and surrounding parishes, 1845

agreed that the children of the Sunday school would only be awarded for reciting Bible verses in Welsh. When, in 1866, the Sunday school superintendent Daniel Thomas suggested that the younger children should be taught in English, this was fortunately not followed.

Table: Places of worship that opened, 1841–61

Name & location	Denomination	Established	Language, 1841–61
St Peter's, City Rd	Catholic	1861	English
Tredegarville	Baptist	1861	English
Gilgal, Llandaff	C.M.	1857	Welsh
Hope, Canton	Baptist	1851	English

St John's, Canton	Church of England	1854	English
Salem, Adamsdown	Baptist	1861	Welsh
Bethesda, Tongwynlais	Independent	1861	Welsh
Salem, Tongwynlais	Baptist	1860	English
Hermon, Tongwynlais	C.M.	1859	Welsh
Siloam, Butetown	Baptist	1857	Welsh
St Michael's, Tongwynlais	Church of England	1860	English
Conwy Rd, Canton	Wesleyan	1859	English
Bronllwyn, Pentyrch	Independent	1858	Welsh
St Mary's, Butetown	Church of England	1845	English
St David's, town	Catholic	1842	English
Beulah, Rhiwbina	Independent	1848	Welsh
Holl Seintiau Newydd, Newtown	Church of England	1856	Welsh
Hope, town	Baptist	1851	English
Bethania, Butetown	C.M.	1853	Welsh
Salem, Canton	C.M.	1856	Welsh
Mount Stuart, Butetown	Independent	1856	Welsh
Charles Street, town	Independent	1853	English
Llandaff Rd, Canton	Baptist	1853	Welsh

CHAPTER 6

From Promotion to Expulsion

THE ACKNOWLEDGEMENT OF the need for educational training was the greatest cultural change of the 16th century. There was certainly a higher demand, with education becoming essential to the ambitious as well as to those who wanted to emulate the new image of men of the Reformation. In the short term at least, the Reformation did no damage to the Welsh language and provided the Bible through the medium of Welsh in 1588. Sir Edward Stradling (1529–1609) set the foundations to create a grammar school in Cowbridge and bore the cost of 1,250 copies of Siôn Dafydd Rhys' Welsh grammar, *Cambrobrytanicae Linguae Institutiones*, in 1592. Some of the gentry employed teachers to teach their children at home. For example, the widow of Lewis y Fan employed three teachers so that her son was taught Latin, French and Welsh. Sir Dafydd Mathew, on the other hand, bequeathed money to sustain a school in Llandaff for 20 poor children in the 15th century. Similarly, in Cardiff also, there was a school taught by John John who dwelt in Crocerton, and Rhys Meurig refers to the existence of schools in Llandaff and Cardiff in 1576.

In 1649/50, during the Cromwellian era, what could be described as the first Education Act was passed, entitled 'An Act for the better propagation and preaching of the Gospel in Wales'. Several schools were set up in Wales; eight in Glamorgan, with one being in Cardiff with Andrew Bancroft as the master. The schools were closed after the restoration of the monarchy in 1660. In 1674, Thomas Gouge started a movement in Wales for the advancement of Puritan principles. Another of his aims was to teach poor children in Wales to read and write in English. The movement came to an end around 1690.

In 1707, the will of Jane Herbert from Cardiff, who was described as a spinster of Whitefriars, called for the establishment of a Free School for 15 children of poor parents. Three years later, the will of Craddock Wells bequeathed money towards the education and upbringing of the many poor boys and girls in the town of Cardiff. In 1777, the schools of Jane Herbert and Craddock Wells were merged. Four years later, in 1781, the minutes record a payment of £7.4s. being made to a John Jones, 'ye school master' of the charity school. It seems that John Jones remained as the schoolmaster of the Craddock Wells school until he died in 1792.

During this period thousands of Welsh books were printed and distributed to schools, as Welsh was probably the only language of 90% of the children at the time. Despite this, English was the only language used in the above schools and, as a result, the teaching was not very effective. The Church records also show that the distribution of the books was not perfect. For example Leckwith, which did not have a school, received the books, whilst the Cardiff school had none. Stephen Hughes, the publisher from Carmarthen, insisted that Church schools should be teaching children through the medium of their home language, which made their lessons more fruitful.

The following references from the St John's Parish Register support the existence of a series of schoolteachers in the town of Cardiff between 1682 and 1763:

1682 – Elizabeth, daughter of Thomas Price, schoolmaster, was buried
1711 – Thomas Price was buried
1732 – Alice, wife of George Williams, schoolmaster, buried
1733 – Elizabeth, daughter of Richard Price, schoolmaster, buried

1740 – Dissenting teacher paid two shillings, seven and a half pence
1742 – Mary, daughter of Wm Miles, schoolmaster, baptised
1763 – Ann, daughter of John Jones, the schoolteacher, died

In 1698 the Society for the Promotion of Christian Knowledge (SPCK) was established, with the Rev. James Harris, the vicar of Llantrisant and a canon at Llandaff, as its main clerical supporter in Wales. The SPCK tried to inspire people to make charitable gifts to sustain schools. As a result, as mentioned earlier, a school was maintained in Cardiff with the charity of Jane Herbert and Craddock Wells, and a school serving the parishes of Llanishen and Lisvane through the charity of Mary Lewis (1728). Another school was opened thanks to the generosity of the Rev. John Cooke at St Fagans. The SPCK operated the same language policy as the Welsh Trust: to promote Welsh literature but to teach through the medium of English. As early as 1705/6, the Bishop of Hereford had 68 Welsh books, 58 that had been printed by the SPCK and the others were translations. In 1725 William Morgan, one of the choral vicars of Llandaff, received 35 Welsh Bibles from the SPCK that were paid for by Thomas Davies, also of Llandaff.

It would appear that the school started by Sir Dafydd Mathew in 1470 was still in existence in 1817 when a church school was opened there. There is no reason not to believe that the schools established in Cardiff, Llanishen and Lisvane and St Fagans had continued throughout the 18th century, becoming church schools in the next century. The SPCK's Welsh books, though used generally, were not welcomed in Llantwit Major where the vicar in 1725 complained that his parishioners did not speak Welsh.

In the same year there was a collection of SPCK Welsh books in Cardiff gaol and, in 1741, one of the prisoners had his own copy of *Dyletswydd Dyn* (The duties of man), *Canwyll y Cymry* (The candle of the Welsh) and the Welsh Bible. Even in 1862 the chaplain of Cardiff prison said: 'I would not have considered myself competent to fully discharge my duties efficiently unless I was fully able to read, write and speak fluently in the Welsh language.' Thomas Price of Merthyr and Llandaff was responsible for making sure that all prisons in Wales had copies of all of the SPCK's Welsh books. Price died in 1729, and in the same way that he had promoted the work of Stephen Hughes, the publisher from Carmarthen, in supporting the Welsh language in education, so too did Griffith Jones, Llanddowror. He was elected a member of the SPCK in 1713 when he was 29 years of age. After this he corresponded regularly with the Society up to his death in 1761. He, through his circulatory schools, was a strong supporter of Welsh-medium education.

Between 1738 and 1773, 29 circulatory schools, catering for over 900 scholars, were set up in the area of what we now recognise as Cardiff, and taught through the medium of Welsh. Immediately beyond the boundary to the east there lay a string of villages, stretching from Marshfield to Michaelstone-y-Fedw, where there were schools which Madam Bevan and Griffith Jones frequently visited. On the north and west sides of the area, the picture was the same from St Nicholas to St Andrews, from Eglwys Ilan to Efail Isaf and from Groes-wen to Groes-faen. Forty Welsh circulatory schools were set up in these small areas and attended by 1,795 pupils: in total there were 2,700 attending 69 different schools and churches. Appendix C gives a list of the schools with the number of pupils on the register indicated in brackets. The map overleaf shows the locations and years of the schools.

In 1767/8, a circulatory school was held in Glamorgan at a church named St John's. The attendance at this unidentified church was less than 20, compared to a church in Swansea of the same name where the class was over a hundred. The Rev. Owen Jenkins was the vicar of St John's, Cardiff, at a time when the Welsh language was predominant in the town.

107

Furthermore, the surrounding parishes all had visits from the circulatory schools, except Caerau and Michaelston-super-Ely whose combined populations were under a hundred and could be served by the circulatory schools of nearby larger parishes. One can only speculate as to whether the unidentified St John's church was that of the Rev. Owen Jenkins.

Griffith Jones bequeathed to Madam Bevan, his chief patron and adviser, the funds of the schools and his private fortune totalling £7,000. She carried on the work of the circulatory schools very successfully until her death in 1779. Indeed, the year 1773, with its 242 schools and 13,205 pupils, was the most successful in the history of the movement. Wales had one of the highest literacy rates in Europe and by 1764 news of the success of these schools had reached Catherine the Great in Russia, who ordered her ministers to make enquires about the scheme.

The annual school reports, called *Welch Piety*, were described as follows:

> An Account of the Circulating Welsh Charity Schools from September 1738 to August 1739. Wherein Men, Women and Children (being ignorant of the English tongue) are taught to Read God's Holy Word in their native British Language. Catechised, and Instructed daily in the Principles and Duties of Religion, for four or five, or sometimes six months, or longer, as those who desire to learn have need of them; and at such times in the year which the Poor can best spare from their Labours to attend them; supported by the Charitable Benefactions of the Well-disposed.

It is a shame that a statue of Griffith Jones was not erected in Cardiff's City Hall despite gaining far more votes in a public competition than both Henry VII and the torturer, Sir Thomas Picton. A letter in the *Western Mail* in July 1913 asked, 'Why include Henry VII who can justly be called a Frenchman as a Welshman, and General Picton in the list? What achievement for Wales can be placed to their credit?'

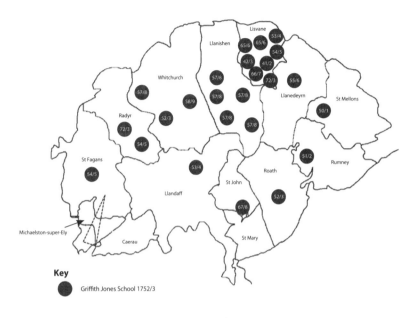

Map: Griffith Jones circulatory schools in Cardiff

With the death of Madam Bevan, the circulatory schools came to an end and even though the Sunday schools gradually made new educational provision, it was scarce before the 19th century. Early in that century, two voluntary movements in England were set up to promote education for poor children: The British and Foreign Schools Society in 1808, and the National Schools Society three years later in 1811. The first was a Nonconformist movement and the other taught in accordance with the religious principles of the Church of England. Both societies used the 'monitors' system to teach the children and many of these 'teachers' took advantage of their experience to open their own private schools. By 1846, in Cardiff and the surrounding parishes, there were as many as 36 schools, 19 of which were private. However, this time, there weren't any characters such as Stephen Hughes, Thomas Price, Griffith Jones and Madam Bevan to campaign for education through the medium of Welsh. From 1833 onwards, the two educational movements received finance from the Government and, of the 36 schools that were in the area, 26 of them had opened after that funding became available. Welsh-medium schools were not funded, and the opportunity to support the successful Griffith Jones circulatory schools was completely ignored. Six of the surrounding parishes did not have a day-school in 1846, whilst Cardiff town had 23 day-schools with over 1,100 pupils, serving a total population of about 15,000. Teachers were paid according to their pupils' results and, as all the tests were in English, the staff had a monetary incentive to rid their pupils of their Welsh as soon as they could. All of these schools taught only through the medium of English and one can imagine the pressure on the children and their families to forget their Welsh so that they could 'get on in the world'.

R.R.W. Lingen, one of the Government's commissioners on the Report of Commission of Enquiry into the State of Education in Wales (1847), known as the Blue Books, described the town as follows: 'From the tradespeople upwards English is spoken, and by the children generally of all classes, unless in families just fresh from the country, but Welsh is still prevalent in the adult labouring classes.' Therefore, it can be seen that there was a social divide, with the working classes remaining Welsh speaking whilst the middle class upwards had turned to English.

One of Lingen's assistants, David Lewis, said in reference to the nearby parishes of Cogan, Llandough, Leckwith and Lavernock: 'Welsh was still in great measure the language of every-day life, but from the number of English families settled in the county, parents found that their children could not get places without speaking English.' Again, the pressure on families to adopt the English language as the language of the home must have been great.

In 1846 Welsh was used in day-schools to explain English books in the parishes of Llanishen, Llanedeyrn and Pentyrch. The Blue Books gives an insight into how Nonconformists and the Established Church treated religious education from the standpoint of the Welsh language. Of the nine Sunday schools that were held in Established Church buildings, not one used the Welsh language as a medium of education. It therefore appears that no use was made of Welsh in Sunday schools, such as in Llanishen, though it was used in their day-school to help the children. Furthermore, Welsh was used exclusively in church services in Lisvane, Caerau, Michaelston-super-Ely, Rumney and Llanedeyrn in 1850. Church services alternated between Welsh and English in St Mellons, Radyr, Whitchurch, St Mary's (All Saints) and Pentyrch. In the parishes of Roath, Llandaff and St Fagans, Welsh services ceased around 1840, 1848 and 1850 respectively. The bishops' returns for St John's in town usually ignored the question of the language used in their services.

Table: Day-schools in Cardiff town, St Mary's and St John's parishes, 1846

Description of School	Year Established	Pupils Present	Language used (Welsh or English)
St Mary's parish			
Free Boys (Church)	1814	111*[18]	Eng.
Free Girls (Church)	1814	79	Eng.
Infant (Nonconformist)	1841	120	Eng.
Union (Workhouse)	1835	54	Eng.
Wesleyan (Boys)	1845	75	Eng.
Wesleyan (Girls)	1845	60	Eng.
Miss Cadie's	1845	24	Eng.
Mr Evans	1819	75	Eng.
Miss Gomer's	1844	20	Eng.
Mrs Hochstoff's	1821	19	Eng.
Mrs Lewis'	1837	21	Eng.
Mrs Llewelyn's	1847	9*	Eng.
Roman Catholic	1845	70	Eng.
Mrs Thomas	1833	32	Eng.
Total St Mary's		**769**	

St John's parish

British Boys	1846	95	Eng.
British Girls	1846	109	Eng.
Mrs Bazeley's	1846	18*	Eng.
Mrs Grant's	1845	14	Eng.
Mrs Kerr's	1842	57	Eng.
Mrs Lloyd's	1843	13	Eng.
Miss Meredith	1845	30	Eng.
Miss Thomas	1845	11	Eng.
Mrs Lewis	1845	38	Eng.
Total St John's		**385**	
Grand total for town		**1,154**	

Table: Day-schools in the surrounding parishes and those without schools, 1846

Llandaff (National Boys)	1817	48	Eng.
Llandaff (National Girls)	1817	50	Eng.
Llandaff, Mrs Williams	1847	4	No details given
Llandaff, Mr Williams	Refused to give details		
Llanedeyrn, Pen-y-Groes	1847	10*	Welsh/Eng.
Llanishen, New House (Church)	1827	39	Eng.
Llanishen village (Church)	1827	36	Welsh/Eng.
St Fagans, Lady Clive's (Church)	1846	64	Eng.
St Fagans, Mrs Evans (Church)	1846	17*	Eng.
Whitchurch (Miss Crea's)	1839	21	Eng.
Whitchurch (Miss Jordan's)	1837	28	Eng.
Whitchurch village (private)	1821	32	Eng.
Michaelston-super-Ely		No school	
Caerau		No school	
Radyr		No school	
Llysfaen		No school	
Roath village (Church)	1836	25	Eng.

Pentyrch (Church)	1834	56	Eng.
Total		**430**	

The parishes of Rumney and St Mellons were not included in the inspection of the Blue Books, but both parish churches held their services mainly in Welsh into the second half of the 19th century, whilst the four local Nonconformist chapels held their services in Welsh to the end of the century.

In Pentyrch, its four Nonconformist chapels held their services in Welsh well into the 20th century, in sharp contrast to the parish church which held its Sunday school in English as early as 1834. Bethlehem, in Gwaelod-y-Garth, is still a thriving Welsh-language chapel today.

Table: Sunday schools in Cardiff town, 1846

Description of School	Year Established	Pupils Present	Language used (Welsh or English)
St John's parish			
St John's	1835	102	Eng.
Ebeneser (Independent)	1827	102	Welsh/Eng.
Trinity (Womanby Street)	1846	55	Eng.
Seion (Calvinistic Methodist)	1814	110	Welsh
St Mary's parish[19]			
St Mary's	1844	95	Eng./Welsh
Bethany Baptist	1813	150	Eng.
Tabernacl Welsh Baptist	1835	116	Eng./Welsh
Glass House Baptist	1840	60	Eng.
Catholic	1844	180	Eng.
Total Welsh of two parishes		291 (30%)	
Total English of two parishes		679 (70%)	
Grand total		**970**	

The process of downgrading the Welsh language when dealing with the needs of Sunday school children was not confined to the Established Church. Of the three Welsh chapels in the town around 1814, 1827 and 1835, only Seion used Welsh alone, whilst Ebeneser and Tabernacl used English and Welsh in their Sunday schools.

CHAPTER 7

The Turning Point

The growth of Cardiff

Bristol's population, estimated by the Hearth Tax of 1670, was 14,500, whilst in the same year, using the same basis for estimating, the population of Cardiff and its surrounding parishes was 5,700. Thus, the population of Bristol was then two and a half times greater than that of Cardiff. The increase in population was due to Bristol trading with America between 1564 and 1671. The early years of the 18th century saw further rapid expansion of the West Indies trade, when the population of Bristol reached around 45,500 (though that figure remained almost static until a further upturn around 1760 to an estimated figure of 55,000). When the first census was held in 1801, Bristol's population had reached 63,000, whilst that of the Cardiff area was only 6,348. However, after the American War of Independence, Bristol did not recover from the ensuing decline in its trade with America, and its West Indies slave trade was surpassed by that of Liverpool at the beginning of the 19th century. In contrast, this was the century of incredible growth for Cardiff, one which would eventually lead to city and capital status.

The iron industry had planted roots in the Cardiff area as far back as 1720. An iron furnace had been opened at Melingriffith, and by 1759 it was joined by a tinplate works. There was also a small copper works in the town, near the West Gate. In addition to the Cardiff–Bristol trade, the arrival of the Industrial Revolution strengthened the commercial and social links between the Cardiff area and the Welsh Valleys where substantial industrial developments at Merthyr were destined to have a revolutionary and lasting effect upon the small port. Goods from America had also started to have an influence on the trade and habits of the people. A report from 1752 noted that at least a hundred little shops, close to the ports of Cardiff, Newport and Aberthaw, were selling tobacco and being managed mainly by people who could speak Welsh but not understand English.

The opening of the Glamorganshire Canal in 1794 and its extension to Sea Lock in 1798 spurred the growth of the town and the surrounding parishes. By 1831 the area's population had reached a total of 12,634. In 1835, four years before the opening of the Bute Dock, approximately 150,000 tons of coal were exported almost exclusively to coastal destinations. When the first dock was opened in October 1839, and the Cardiff to Merthyr railway in 1841, the canal companies, ironmasters and coal exporters were ready to take advantage of the new facilities. Companies such as those at Dowlais, Penydarran, Cyfarthfa, Pentrebach (the Plymouth Works), Melingriffith, Aberdare and smaller yet flourishing companies such as those of Thomas Powell, William Jenkins, Morgan Thomas and Walter Coffin were poised with their established wharfs on the canal to adapt themselves to handle the delivery of goods through the West Junction Canal and other feeders. This enabled the contents of barges to cross under Bute Street and unload their cargos directly onto waiting ships. Alternatively, the canal was still widely used in conjunction with the river and Thomas Powell's coal loading stage operated from 1830 to 1859.

The migration into the town between 1800 and 1835 was largely from the southern counties of Wales. This is corroborated, as is mentioned in chapter five, by the language of the 24 new places of worship in the town and in the parishes.

116

Twenty-two of these conducted their services wholly in Welsh, one partly so, and one in English. Had there been a language census in 1840, it would have revealed that in each of the surrounding parishes there was a majority of Welsh speakers with a sizeable Welsh-speaking population in the town itself. During this period, Cardiff's population surpassed the population of surrounding parishes, based on census returns, as is shown below.

Table: Population of Cardiff and surrounding parishes, 1801–41

Year	1801	1811	1821	1831	1841
Cardiff	1,870	2,457	3,521	6,187	10,077
Surrounding parishes	4,562	4,903	5,762	6,447	7,078
Total	**6,432**	**7,360**	**9,283**	**12,634**	**17,155**

The 1851 census recorded a growth in the town's population from 10,077 (in 1841) to 18,351, although just over 2,000 of these were counted as being on board ships in the docks, on the canal, or anchored in the river or bay. A study of the 16,259 residing in the town shows a growing number of incomers, many having come from Glamorgan and the rest of Wales, whilst others came from the West of England, and Ireland.

The table below notes the birthplaces of the people who resided in Cardiff as recorded in the 1851 census. As was shown in chapter five, the increase of people born outside of Wales led to the opening of 11 English places of worship between 1845 and 1861.

Table: Origin of Cardiff's population, 1851

Total	Glamorgan	Rest of Wales	All Wales	England	Ireland	Others
16,259	7,437	2,188	9,625	3,901	2,363	370
%	45.8	13.4	59.2	24.0	14.5	2.3

The period of boom

The 1861 census of the town shows the population more than doubling from 16,259 to 32,954. A thorough analysis of that census reveals the composition of the town's population. The breakdown identifies Wales, the English West Country and Ireland, respectively, as the main places of origin of the residents of the town and its emerging suburbs of Roath, Canton and Grangetown. The surrounding parishes, as yet, had absorbed only small numbers of incomers.

The Irish came onto the scene post-1835, shortly after the commencement of the work on the Bute West Dock. It was said that in 1820 only two Irishmen lived in Cardiff and both were fluent Welsh speakers. The Irish famine of the late 1840s and the changes brought about by the opening of the East Dock resulted in a large increase in the Irish presence. The conditions that some of these immigrants had to endure were horrendous. The Rammel Report, initiated by the health board to examine the health and sanitary conditions in Cardiff, noted that 54 Irish people lived, slept and ate in one room in 17 Stanley Street. These conditions led to the Irish undercutting Welsh labourers and that caused tensions between them. There was serious conflict between Cardiff's Welsh and Irish communities in November 1848 after Thomas Lewis, a 30-year-old collier and the son of William Lewis, the publican of the Red Lion, was stabbed to death by an Irishman named John Connors. The police failed to arrest the assailant immediately and, in their rage, several thousand people attacked St David's Catholic Church. The priest, Father Millea, fled for his life and did not return.

According to the 1851 census, around 15% of the population of Cardiff were Irish, with the majority coming from Cork and Waterford. Migration from the western counties of England accounted for 24% of the town's population by 1851. The Rhymney railway line to Cardiff became operational in 1858 and, together with the opening of the Bute East Dock in 1859, drew thousands of newcomers to the town and the surrounding parishes. By analysing the 1861 census for birthplace information, a clearer picture of the composition of the town can be revealed. It is already clear that there was a population shift, wherein people who had worked on the land now found themselves learning new skills that made them appropriate for maritime or industrial work. In seeking to uncover the structure of Cardiff's population, an analysis becomes more informative by counting children, together with their parents. Tables consisting of eight columns were used to note the numbers in each group:

Column 1 lists those who are from Wales and their children as **Welsh**
Column 2 lists those from Wales and England as **Anglo/Welsh**
Column 3 lists members of mixed Welsh and Irish families as **Welsh/Irish**
Column 4 lists the English born and their families as **English**
Column 5 lists those from England and Ireland as **Anglo/Irish**
Column 6 lists the Irish born and their families as **Irish**
Column 7 lists those not in any of the above groups as **'Others'**
Column 8 shows **the sum totals** enumerated in each specific group

Parts of the 1861 census have been lost but they represent only a very small fraction of the census record. The analysis of the 1861 census is composed of three areas of Cardiff town, two town areas of Irish predominance, two areas of Butetown, the emerging suburbs of Roath, Canton and Grangetown, Whitchurch, Llandaff and Pentyrch, as well as nine smaller parishes: Rumney, St Mellons, Llanedeyrn, St Fagans, Caerau, Radyr, Michaelson-super-Ely, Llanishen and Lisvane.

Table: An Analysis of the town's population in 1861 according to place of origin

Welsh	W/E	W/I	English	E/I	Irish	Others	Total
11,921	3,432	271	10,027	334	5,867	1,160	33,012
36.2%	10.4%	0.8%	30.4%	1%	17.8%	3.52%	100%

The numbers of Welsh, Anglo-Welsh and Welsh/Irish totalled 15,624 (47.4%). Whereas, the combination of the English group and the Anglo/Irish group totalled 10,361(31.4%) and the Irish group totalled 5,867 (17.8%). Though the joint Welsh groups (Welsh, Anglo-Welsh and Irish/Welsh) were the predominant group, the in-migration from England and Ireland seemed poised to overtake the Welsh.

Table: Population of Cathays, Tredegarville, High St, Union Buildings and Wharton St, 1861

Welsh	W/E	W/I	English	E/I	Irish	Others	Total
2,276	430	38	1,367	71	526	104	4,812
47.3%	8.94%	0.79%	28.41%	1.48%	10.93%	2.16%	100%

Combined Welsh population rows: 1, 2 & 3: 2,744 (57.03%)

Table: Population of Charles St, Baker's Row, St Mary's St, Edward St and Gt Frederick St, 1861

Welsh	W/E	W/I	English	E/I	Irish	Others	Total
2,150	697	23	1,251	30	552	110	4,813
44.7%	14.5%	0.48%	26.0%	0.60%	11.5%	2.22%	100%

Combined Welsh population: rows 1, 2 & 3: 2,870 (59.68%)

Table: Population of Caroline St, Charlotte St, Court Colman Row, Scott St and Wood St, 1861

Welsh	W/E	W/I	English	E/I	Irish	Others	Total
2,136	600	55	1,322	136	630	110	4,989
43%	12.05%	1.1%	26.5%	2.6%	12.7%	2.05%	100%

Combined Welsh population rows 1, 2 & 3: 2,791 (56.15%)

Newtown

The tables below highlight the concentration of the Irish in and around Newtown on both sides of the railway, sited in 22 streets where they were a considerable majority. These streets north of the railway line were John Street, Whitmore Lane, parts of Bute Terrace, Rodney Street, Rhiwperra Street, Pellet Street, Noah Street, Garth Street, Dyffryn Street, Canal Street, Mary Ann Street, Stanley Street, David Street, Little Frederick Street and Love Lane. To the south of the main railway were Herbert Street, Tyndall Street, Rosemary Street, North William Street, Roland Street, Ellen Street, and Thomas' Court. In total, there were 3,813 Irish men, women and children in these two areas, forming 39.5% of the overall population of 9,624. In addition to these streets was Landore Court (Cwrt Glandŵr), sited between the Guild Hall and the old fire station on the corner of Quay Street. It backed onto the old bed of the River Taff and held around 500 Irish inhabitants, rivalling Stanley Street for its squalid conditions.

The Welsh, Anglo-Welsh and Welsh/Irish elements totalled 3,235 (33.88%) and the English and the Anglo-Irish, 2,304 (23.94%).

The 'Others' totalled 272 (2.86%), signalling the emergence of a cosmopolitan presence which was composed mainly of migrants from mainland Europe who had maritime connections.

Table: Population of Newtown: north of the main railway line, 1861

Welsh	W/E	W/I	English	E/I	Irish	Others	Total
1,094	282	33	792	20	1,616	147	3,984
27.5%	7.1%	0.8%	20%	0.5%	40.5%	3.7%	100%

Table: Population of Newtown: south of the main railway line, 1861

Welsh	W/E	W/I	English	E/I	Irish	Others	Total
1,370	391	65	1,463	29	2,197	125	5,640
24.29%	6.93%	1.15%	25.94%	0.51%	38.95%	2.22%	100%

Butetown

The tables below cover the population of Butetown with its 8,731 residents. The Welsh, Anglo-Welsh and Welsh/Irish numbered 3,980 (45.6%) and the English and Anglo-Irish numbered 3,617 (44.5%). The 'Others' numbered 518 (5.93%), unusually ahead of the Irish who numbered only 346 (3.96%). The Welsh/Irish and the English/Irish combined numbered 103 (1.2%). Indeed, the second table includes 137 Irish living in the new area of Grangetown who, when deducted from the Butetown total, left only 209 Irish dwelling in Butetown, i.e. 2.5% of the total inhabitants.

The long maritime tradition along the Severn coast shared by the Welsh and West of England seafarers dominated much of the shipping work around Cardiff Docks. The Irish dwelling in Newtown, however, with its close proximity to the dockside was increasingly prominent amongst the dock workers. In the early years the Welsh, with their experience of handling coal, dominated coal trimming.[20] The last group of Welsh-speaking trimmers worked as a gang of eight up to the outbreak of the Second World War. The relationship between the trimmers and the shipping and mining companies was generally very good, with disputes being short-lived. In the 1891 census, 220 (34%) of the coal trimmers were Welsh speaking, with the great majority being born in Pentyrch, the town itself or in the Vale of Glamorgan. Among those who were not Welsh-speaking Welshmen, there were some who were married to Welsh-speaking wives or who lodged with Welsh speakers or who, as did four Irishmen and two Englishmen, learned Welsh. In 1890/91, 18 of the 40 who represented the trimmers on their union committee were Welsh speaking. It is incredible to think that during this time one of the bastions of the Welsh language in Cardiff would have been amongst the black dust in the bowels of coal ships. It was in 1890 that Cardiff surpassed New York City as the busiest exporting port in the world.

Table: Population of Butetown east, 1861

Welsh	W/E	W/I	English	E/I	Irish	Others	Total
1,448	501	25	1,851	33	117	240	4,215
34.3%	11.9%	0.6%	43.9%	0.8%	2.8%	5.7%	100%

Table: Population of Butetown west, 1861

Welsh	W/E	W/I	English	E/I	Irish	Others	Total
1,450	531	25	1,983	20	229	278	4,516
31.8%	11.8%	0.55%	44%	0.4%	5.35%	6.15%	100%

From Villages to Suburbs

The expansion of the town into the villages of Canton, Roath and Grangetown had by 1861 made provision for 1,235 new houses, catering for almost 7,000 people.

Table: Total population of suburbs (Roath, Canton & Grangetown), 1861[21]

Welsh	W/E	W/I	English	E/I	Irish	Others	Total
2,237	818	55	2,619	46	859	159	6,793
33%	12%	1%	39%	1%	13%	2%	100%

In Roath, the pattern of growth was much the same as that in Butetown: the combined total of the Welsh and the Anglo-Welsh at 1,390 forming 47.55% of the population. The English population, at 1,124, represented 38.4% of the inhabitants. The 323 Irish were 11% of the new community.

123

Table: Population of Roath, 1861

Welsh	W/E	W/I	English	E/I	Irish	Others	Total
1,023	367	1	1,124	10	323	78	2,926
35%	12.55%	0.03 %	38.4%	0.34%	11%	2.7%	100%

Canton

The combined total of the Welsh, Welsh/Irish and Anglo-Welsh groups was 1,741, forming 43.56% of the population. The English and English/Irish groups at 1,555 (39.55%) were also a substantial proportion of the population. The Irish presence at 543 (13.85%) was larger than the Irish numbers in Roath, as also were the numbers of mixed Irish and Welsh, and English and Irish marriages at 92 (2.3%).

Table: Population of Canton, 1861

Welsh	W/E	W/I	English	E/I	Irish	Others	Total
1,230	456	55	1,518	37	543	81	3,920
31.5%	11.66%	1.4%	38.65%	0.9%	13.85%	2.1%	100%

Grangetown

By 1861 Grangetown's first streets had been built in a triangular shape, bounded by North Clive Street, Havelock Place and Penarth Road. For the purpose of the census, Grangetown formed part of the rapidly expanding suburb of Canton, although its detached location on the Morfa made it easier to analyse the make-up of the community.

Table: Population of Grangetown, 1861

Welsh	W/E	W/I	English	E/I	Irish	Others	Total
119	–	–	208	–	137	–	464
26.66%			44.82%		29.52%		100%

Migration to the surrounding parishes of Llandaff, Pentyrch and Whitchurch, 1861

The following three parishes stand out amongst the others, each having a substantial and growing population.

Llandaff

Of the three, Llandaff, as the diocese centre of Glamorgan and Gwent, had the longer history and presence. Its population in 1801 was 860 and had reached 1,300 by 1831. It also served as the church of the parish of Llandaff, including its chapelries of Fairwater, Ely, Caerau, Mynachdy and Whitchurch. The estate of the Lordship of Llandaff embraced the city of Llandaff, the hamlets of Llandaff North (Ystumtaf), Gabalfa, Fairwater, Caerau, Ely, and the village of Canton. By 1861, Llandaff's population was 2,001, of which 65.25% were Welsh, Anglo-Welsh or Welsh/Irish, whilst almost a third, some 654 individuals, were born in England.

Table: Population of Llandaff, 1861

Welsh	W/E	W/I	English	E/I	Irish	Others	Total
1,101	196	5	654	–	27	19	2,001
55%	10%	0.25%	33%	–	1%	1%	100%

Pentyrch

In 1861, some 95% of the inhabitants of Pentyrch were Welsh or Anglo-Welsh, whilst the remaining 5% were composed of 99 migrants from England and 18 from Ireland. Mining was the attraction for most of the workforce, whilst some who were employed as coal trimmers at Cardiff's docks travelled daily back and forth using railway trucks for their transport. The population grew from 470 in 1801, to 747 in 1821, to 1,248 in 1841 and to 2,235 by 1861. The village had no less than five Welsh-medium Nonconformist chapels and a bilingual Established Church.

125

Table: Population of Pentyrch, 1861

Welsh	W/E	W/I	English	E/I	Irish	Others	Total
1,992	126	–	99	–	18	–	2,235
89.3%	5.65%	–	4.4%	–	0.8%	–	100%

Whitchurch

Again, the Welsh and Anglo-Welsh formed the bulk of the population at 86.35%. The English and Anglo-Irish represented almost an eighth of the inhabitants, whilst 33 Irish formed just 1.5% of the residents. The Melingriffith works provided the main source of employment. The population, which was just under 700 in 1801, increased to 1,376 by 1841 and to 2,252 by 1861. A quote from the 1847 Blue Books, referring to Whitchurch, claims that 'English is spoken principally in this neighbourhood'. This statement is in stark contrast to other evidence. Of the ten places of worship opened in Whitchurch and Tongwynlais between 1808 and 1861, nine were Welsh medium and the only English one had the smallest gathering. The parish church held its services bilingually, and analysis of the 1891 census shows that in Whitchurch all of those that were born in the area and over the age of 65 spoke Welsh. In 1857 Thomas Carlyle, the Scottish historian and writer, said: 'Eglwys Newydd, New Church as the Welsh peasants still name it, though officially it is now called White Church.' It was possible also at the time for English families to become assimilated and adopt the Welsh language. In 1851, William Shapland, George Shapland, John Steel and James Brookman are listed as living near the railway station in Whitchurch and all were born in England. However, by 1891, their descendants, still living in the same street with the same surnames, are listed as Welsh speakers.

Table: Population of Whitchurch, 1861

Welsh	W/E	W/I	English	E/I	Irish	Others	Total
1,767	177	–	272	1	33	2	2,252
78.53%	7.85%	–	12.0%	0.04%	1.51%	0.08%	100%

Lesser populated parishes, 1861

St Mellons

The population of St Mellons ranged from 451 in 1801 to 564 in 1831 and to 688 by 1861. The Welsh and the Anglo-Welsh formed 88.5% of the population whilst the remainder were occupied by 72 English and eight Irish residents.

Table: Population of St Mellons, 1861

Welsh	W/E	W/I	English	E/I	Irish	Others	Total
570	38	–	72	–	8	–	688
83%	5.5%	–	10.45%	–	1.05%	–	100%

St Fagans

In the 1847 Blue Books, in reference to the state of education in Wales, it is noted, 'that such labour as is done in the parish is agricultural. This work is carried out by the very old and very young and the rate of wages is 12*s.* per week. The young and able-bodied [of St Fagans] work either at the docks at Cardiff, or in the Pentyrch works: hence much debauchery is introduced into the parish.' It was the assumption of the contributors to the Blue Books that Pentyrch men working at Cardiff Docks would inevitably bring bad habits back to villages such as St Fagans. By 1885 it was said in the *Goleuad*, the Methodist Calvinistic weekly newspaper, that many of the young people of St Fagans went to the parish church as they could not understand the Welsh services at Tabernacl in the village.

Table: Population of St Fagans, 1861

Welsh	W/E	W/I	English	E/I	Irish	Others	Total
301	42	–	64	–	25	9	441
68.30%	9.5%	–	14.5%	–	5.65%	2.05%	100%

Radyr

Radyr's population doubled from 227 in 1831 to 505 by 1861. This increase was largely brought about by the arrival of the

Taff Vale railway line. Agricultural labourers left the land to get better pay on the railways, leaving farming jobs for Irish and English migrants to fill. In 1906, Jane Watkins, born in Radyr in 1825, gave her evidence in court in Welsh through an interpreter.

Table: Population of Radyr, 1861

Welsh	W/E	W/I	English	E/I	Irish	Others	Total
400	32	4	29	–	33	7	505
79.25%	6.35%	0.8%	5.75%	–	6.55%	1.3%	100%

Llanishen

Llanishen's population varied little between 329 in 1801 and 380 in 1861. It had a strong Welsh base and a combined English and Irish presence numbering 73 in all.

Table: Population of Llanishen, 1861

Welsh	W/E	W/I	English	E/I	Irish	Others	Total
304	–	3	56	3	14	–	380
80%	–	0.8%	14.7%	0.8%	3.7%	–	100%

Rumney

The population of Rumney in 1801 was 235, 305 in 1841 and 356 by 1861. The Welsh and Anglo-Welsh formed 86% of the residents, with the English at 7.5% and the Irish at 6.5%. The growth of Rumney began in 1841, coinciding with the opening of the first dock and the Taff Vale Railway. By 1861, following the opening of the second dock and prior to that the Rhymney Valley line, there was a further small increase in the village's population. The Irish were almost ever-present and presumably found ready work in agricultural areas such as Rumney.

Table: Population of Rumney, 1861

Welsh	W/E	W/I	English	E/I	Irish	Others	Total
250	56	–	27	–	23	–	356
70.25%	15.75%	–	7.5%	–	6.5%	–	100%

Llanedeyrn

Llanedeyrn's population varied little between 1801 and 1861, going from 301 to 291. Even as late as 1901, it still had only 291 residents. The presence of 18 English and six Irish would have brought new faces and a new language to the sparsely populated parish. It is likely that migration of locals to Cardiff and Merthyr would explain the parish's static appearance.

Table: Population of Llanedeyrn, 1861

Welsh	W/E	W/I	English	E/I	Irish	Others	Total
240	26	–	18	1	6	–	291
82.5%	8.95%	–	6.2%	0.3%	2.05%	–	100%

Lisvane

Lisvane, with an even smaller population than Llanedeyrn, must have regarded the arrival of 14 Irish and nine English people as being a minor invasion. The parish's population appears to have been static, having 221 residents in 1801 and increasing slightly in 1861 to 226.

Table: Population of Lisvane, 1861

Welsh	W/E	W/I	English	E/I	Irish	Others	Total
194	9	–	9	–	14	–	226
86%	4%	–	4%	–	6%	–	100%

Caerau

Of Caerau's 133 residents, 80 were Welsh or Anglo-Welsh with the remainder being 33 Irish and 20 English people. For such a small parish, its sudden diversity must have come as quite a shock. Its population was just 43 in 1811 and only increased to 80 in 1841.

Table: Population of Caerau, 1861

Welsh	W/E	W/I	English	E/I	Irish	Others	Total
73	7	–	20	–	33	–	133
55%	5%	–	15%	–	25%	–	100%

Michaelston-super-Ely

It seems that even the smallest of parishes received at least one Irish exile, and that nine English migrants suddenly became a fifth of the population in the small parish of Michaelston-super-Ely in 1861.

Table: Population of Michaelston-super-Ely, 1861

Welsh	W/E	W/I	English	E/I	Irish	Other	Total
37	–	–	9	–	1	–	47
79%	–	–	19%	–	2%	–	100%

Table: Total population of the surrounding parishes in 1861: Llandaff, Pentyrch, Whitchurch, St Mellons, St Fagans, Radyr, Llanishen, Rumney, Llanedeyrn, Lisvane, Caerau, Michaelston-super-Ely

Welsh	W/E	W/I	English	E/I	Irish	Others	Total
7,229	709	12	1,329	5	235	37	9,556
75.65%	7.44%	0.1%	13.9%	0.05%	2.46%	0.35%	100%

In conclusion it can be said that the population of the Welsh, Anglo-Welsh and Welsh/Irish in 1861 totalled 7,950 (83.19%). The population of English and Anglo-Irish totalled 1,334 (13.95%). The population of Irish totalled 235 (2.46%) and each one of the surrounding parishes had a majority of Welsh-born residents.

CHAPTER 8

A Change of Language

THE ENGLISH INFLUENCE increased during the 1860s and was affecting Welsh institutions. Some of this was caused by the voluntary promotion of the English language by Welsh Nonconformist leaders. For instance, in 1866, when Ebeneser chapel was without a minister, the Rev. John Davies went there to persuade them to become an English-medium cause. It was firmly pointed out to him that there was an English-language chapel in the next street and that Ebeneser was established to serve the Welsh-speaking population of Cardiff. John Davies was a strong promoter of the English cause. Whilst a minister at the Mount Stuart Welsh chapel, he established an English chapel nearby in Hannah Street and eventually left in 1868 with a number of members to become its minister.

When the Welsh Independent cause was established in Canton in 1867, it only took three years for the minister, T.C. Williams, to start a campaign to change the language of the chapel. He failed, and therefore left to start an English-language chapel. Except for the Welsh Independent chapel in Canton, only two other Welsh chapels were opened between 1860 and 1880: Salem, Adamsdown (Baptist) in 1861, and Libanus, Roath (Calvinistic Methodist) in 1868, which in fact 12 years later turned into an English-language cause.

The population of the town had reached 39,536 by the census of 1871 and the burgeoning suburbs of Roath, Canton and Grangetown had 7,991 and 9,250 inhabitants respectively, creating within the town an urban mass of 56,777. It is estimated that 80.9% of the people of Cardiff over the age of 14 in 1871 had been born outside the town. Llandaff and Whitchurch showed increases of 660 and 550 respectively, whilst Pentyrch's population of 2,105 appeared to be static at that time, as did that of the nine remaining smaller parishes. Short-distance migration attracted families to move closer to the inner areas of the town and docks, and this census illustrates large numbers of people from Glamorgan and Gwent moving into the town and its new suburbs. Furthermore, families from the West of England arrived in growing numbers, together with a steady influx from Ireland.

By 1871 migration to the town and its emerging suburbs was estimated by cartographer Ernst Georg Ravenstein to have decreased the Welsh-speaking population to around 20%. However, Ravenstein's estimate of the town's Welsh-speaking population excluded the suburbs of Roath, Canton and Grangetown, as these wards were not officially absorbed into the town until 1875. In 1878, Ravenstein calculated the percentage of Welsh speakers in Cardiff as 37.5%, even though the number of Welsh speakers in the expanding suburbs was much lower than those within the old town. This was still a significant percentage but there is no doubt that the Welsh language was being drowned by English and that English was the language of commerce. The situation had changed so much in a few decades that the journalist and American consul in Cardiff, Wirt Sikes, wrote these exaggerated words in his article, 'On the Taff', in 1877:

> No Welsh is heard on the streets of Cardiff. It is preached in
> some pulpits and spoken in some homes, and the most cultivated
> burgesses take pride in their knowledge, be the same more or less,
> of the Welsh language and literature; but for the common uses of
> life the English language is as much the language of Cardiff as it is
> of New York.

One overexcited 'special commissioner' wrote in the *Western Mail* in 1899 that there was more Welsh heard in Wilkes-Barre, Pennsylvania, than in Cardiff. However, Wirt Sikes also wrote that the 12 Welsh-language chapels attracted large congregations:

> In the twelve of the so-called chapels the Welsh tongue is employed and in none of the places of worship could a thin congregation ever be found on a Sunday unless there was a plague in town.

In 1893, in an article entitled 'Vanishing Cardiff Welsh', J. Hobson Mathews, the town's archivist, disagreed with Sikes and said that there was 'plenty of Welsh in Cardiff streets... especially on Saturdays when the country folk come into market or Mondays when the miners and their families invade the town...' However, after reminding readers that Welsh was the 'language of Cardiffian discourse' 70 years ago, he said that the '... old language is becoming yearly scarcerer among us...' and criticised the removal of the inscription *Cymry, ymwelwch â Chymro* (The Welsh, visit a Welshman) from a restaurant in Queen Street. He was also concerned that names such as Pont-y-llechau, the bridge over the Lleucu brook, and Ffynnon Bren, Pant-yr-wyn, Tŷ'n-y-coed and Tŷ'r Ceiliog would be forgotten now that Penylan had become a part of Cardiff. He foresaw that, in 50 years' time, Penylan would be called Penny-land. Professor Prys Morgan has a story about himself searching in Radyr in the 1950s for a well named Pistyll Golau, only to discover that it was now called Pitcher Cooler. J. Hobson Mathews was a prophet, as when I was a child the Lleucu brook was called Roath brook. To rectify that, when my wife Siân started a Welsh-medium nursery in Penylan for my youngest boys and their friends, the nursery was called 'Nant Lleucu'. The nursery still flourishes in 2020 and Lleucu is once again used for the brook that runs through Penylan.

E.F. Kennard, from south-west England, the owner of

the largest bike company in Cardiff, also spoke of the lack of Welsh heard on the streets of Cardiff in his 1918 book, *The Men I Have Known*. He wrote: 'Are there as many Welsh people in Cardiff today as there were in 1867 when I came to reside in Cardiff? Then it was common to hear Welsh people talking on the streets but now you may walk the Cardiff streets from morning until night and not hear a Welsh word spoken.' This was not from a person who was against the Welsh language. He said of the minister of Tabernacl: 'Ever since I have known Charles Davies, I have wished I could understand the Welsh language.' He also said that, 'One of the most remarkable sermons that I have ever heard was in the Cardiff Market in 1867. There were thousands of Welsh people there... it was the first and last Welsh sermon I heard, but never to be forgotten.'

There is no doubt that some Welsh speakers in Cardiff held negative views about the future of the Welsh language. When the Corporation of Cardiff wanted to take possession of part of Seion chapel in town in 1876, many were happy to give up the land, saying *'Gwna'r darn fydd ar ôl y tro i ni'r hen Gymry'* (The land left will do for us old Welshmen). Between 1860 and 1880, only three Welsh Nonconformist chapels were opened in Cardiff, compared to 34 English chapels. In addition, many causes changed languages, including All Saints in 1875, Wesleyans in Ely in 1879, Bethesda Independents in Tongwylais in 1880, and Libanus Calvinistic Methodists in Roath in 1880. Also, when the Tabernacl started a cause in Cathays where they had held a Sunday school since 1849, it was an English cause but with a 'Welsh room' for the substantial Welsh-speaking population in the area. In opening the English cause in Great Frederick Street in 1867, Lewis Edwards, the principal of Bala-Bangor Theological Seminary and a great advocate of English causes, said that the increase in the use of English should be embraced:

> You are all aware the English language is gaining ground in the
> Principality. What are we to do? Are we to yield to this inroad?
> Are we to retire before the power of the English language and
> literature? Are we to hide ourselves in the remotest corners of the
> Principality? No. I for one do not see the necessity for yielding, but
> we take advantage of the spread of the English language; we lay
> hold of it and try to adapt ourselves to the changes that take place
> around us.

The Rev. John Davies, Minister of Mount Stuart's Welsh
Congregational Chapel, declared that as four out of five of
Cardiff's population in 1868 were now able to speak English,
efforts should be made to establish more English chapels
in the town. However, Davies' declaration assumed that
those who spoke both Welsh and English were instinctively
inclined to become English and, as a result, he discounted the
bilingual Welsh. Ravenstein's higher estimate of 37.5%, on
the other hand, clearly placed both monoglot and bilingual
Welsh speakers in Cardiff, and in doing so he maximised
their numbers as opposed to the Rev. John Davies' attempt
to minimise them. Ravenstein's assessment of the decreasing
numbers of Welsh speakers in the new suburbs of Cardiff is
made against the background of considerable migration from
the West of England, and Ireland, and the failure, or rejection,
of local authorities and parents to recognise the potential of
bilingualism.

In 1898, in a letter to *Seren Cymru*, the Welsh Baptist
weekly newspaper, the Rev. D.E. Jenkins said that it was of
great advantage that his successor, the Rev. Robert Lloyd,
changed the language of the Welsh Baptist chapel in Canton
to English. He goes on to say that if the young people did not
want to learn Welsh, then English services should be provided
and that the inevitable must be accepted. Others expressed a
similar view when the Wesleyan chapel in Llandaff ceased to
hold Welsh services in 1891. It is clear that the Rev. Lloyd was
not a supporter of the Welsh language, as he also turned the

language of his next chapel in Castleton to English. Neither it seemed was the Rev. Jenkins, as his grave in Cathays is in English only, and the majority of his funeral was conducted in English so that those who couldn't speak Welsh could follow the service.

However, there were exceptions. In 1884, two Welsh causes were opened in Cathays: Minny Street by the Independents and Horeb by the Calvinistic Methodists (which later became Crwys). Stephen George, a Cathays resident and the first treasurer of Minny Street, challenged the officers of Ebeneser to support a Welsh cause in Cathays by saying six out of the seven causes in Cathays were English and it was important to cater for the Welsh speakers. In the same year the Calvinistic Methodists also opened a Welsh Sunday school in Splott. In 1883, during the centenary celebration of the Welsh Baptist cause in Lisvane, its history was written only in Welsh.

However, the Welsh language was being undermined throughout the town and the following chapels yielded and turned into English causes: Bethesda Calvinistic Methodist in St Mellons in 1888, the Wesleyan chapel in Rumney around 1895, Tabernacl Calvinistic Methodist in Whitchurch in 1896, Beulah Independent in Rhiwbina in 1899, the Wesleyan chapel in Llandaff in 1899 and Llandaff Road Baptist in Canton in 1901. Save for Dewi Sant, no other Established Church conducted services in Welsh.

There was no set pattern for a cause turning to English and often it was a process rather than an event. For example, Ararat in Whitchurch was a bilingual church for 25 years from 1878 with a Welsh service in the morning and English in the evening before abandoning the Welsh services altogether in 1903. There was no real pattern of linguistic change within the membership of the chapels, either. Taking for instance the membership of Llandaff Road Baptist in Canton from the 1891 census, this table shows slippage from one generation to the next, especially in mixed marriages.

Table: The families of Llandaff Road Baptist Chapel, 1891

Children from Welsh-speaking families	Children speaking Welsh
109	41 (37.6%)
Children with one parent speaking Welsh	Children speaking Welsh
35	3 (8.6%)

From the 1891 census we can look at the membership in greater detail. For example, the Howard family, John and Sarah from Wenvoe and Caerau, raised at least six children who were Welsh speaking. Two of their sons were married to local Welsh-speaking women. Both John, aged 34, and James, aged 33, were coal trimmers like their father, and also living in Canton. John raised four children who could speak Welsh, whilst James' children could only speak English.

Founders of the cause, people with ordinary jobs such as Robert John, William Gedrych, Lewis Lewis and John Thomas with their wives, had raised at least 20 children who were Welsh speaking. On the other hand, the great sponsors of the chapel, Thomas and Martha Williams from Fishguard, had

raised four children who could not speak Welsh. Thomas Williams was listed as a Master Mariner and lived in Pembroke House in Conway Road, which has subsequently been demolished and is now a nursing home. His children were all members of the chapel and probably added to the pressure to turn the cause to English and

All that is left of Thomas and Martha Williams' home

137

persuaded other families within the chapel to follow their example.

It is no wonder that Dan Isaac Davies, the founder of the first Welsh language society, Society for the Utilization of the Welsh Language, said that Welsh speakers in Cardiff were as useful as a ladder made out of sand:

> *Rhaff o dywod, mewn rhai ystyriaethau ydyw Cymry Cymraeg.*
> *Y maent yn lluosog o ran nifer, ac yn ddylanwadol yn fynych fel*
> *personau unigol; ond nid ydynt, fel corff o bobl, yn meddu dylanwad*
> *cyfatebol i'w rhif a'u pwys personol.*
>
> (In some instances the Welsh speakers are like a ladder of sand.
> They are numerous in number, and often influential as individuals
> but as a corporate body they do not have the influence comparable
> to their number and personal influence.)

Simon Brookes, the contemporary, provocative Welsh academic and writer, made similar comments in 2002 when he said that despite the numerous members of the Cardiff Welsh-speaking community they have failed to leave a cultural mark.

Some of the prominent Welsh speakers in Cardiff that Dan Isaac Davies might have been referring to were D. Alfred Thomas, Edward Thomas and Robert Hughes.

D. Alfred Thomas was born at Llwyn y Grant Uchaf in Penylan. His father Daniel Thomas came from a Cardiff family and was a prominent businessman there. Daniel Thomas was one of the main contractors who built the West Dock in 1839. He was also responsible for rebuilding Cardiff Bridge in 1859, parts of which can still be seen, and also for building the dock feeder that runs parallel with Edwards Terrace (now named Churchill Way) and still runs today into the East Dock. In 1851 he took over the Llandough Lime Works with which his name was in later years chiefly connected. D. Alfred Thomas lived in Bronwydd on Penylan hill where his family had held an annual fair called 'Ffair Pen-y-lan' according to local tradition. D. Alfred Thomas was a staunch supporter of *Cymru Fydd* (the Welsh Liberal movement, Young Wales) and, as a Member of Parliament (1885–1910) he pressed time and again for the House of Commons to create the position of a Secretary of State for Wales. He was prominent in the building of Welsh national institutions, such as the University of Wales, Cardiff, in 1883. He made a contribution of £10,000 to the Welsh National School of Medicine in 1918 which included the Physiological Department facing Newport Road with its five-storey Gothic towers, dominating with its many embossments and the heads of four prominent men of medicine: Pasteur, Lister, Jenner and Hunter. He was knighted in 1902 and raised to the peerage of Lord Pontypridd in 1912. He died in December 1927 in the opening year of the National Museum of Wales of which he was a founder member and its first president. Despite his busy public life he, like his father before him, was a prominent member of the Tabernacl on The Hayes. He attended the weekly prayer meetings, was the Sunday school superintendent for many years, and served as a deacon. He was the first Nonconformist to be made a peer. His minister at Tabernacl, the Rev. Charles Davies, struggled to call anyone Lord except God. It is said that he overcame this by calling D. Alfred Thomas *'ein brawd yr Arglwydd Pontypridd'* (our brother Lord Pontypridd), with emphasis on the brother and not the Lord.

Running parallel with D. Alfred Thomas' work in Cardiff was that of Edward Thomas, alias Cochfarf (Red beard), who was born in 1853 and moved to Cardiff when he was 35 years old. He was a Welsh Baptist, a teetotaller and a carpenter who worked on the building of the Town Hall before turning his business to that of running three coffee taverns: the Gordon Coffee Tavern on the corner of Bute Street and Custom House Street, the Metropole which was located under the bridge of the Taff Vale Railway, and the Red Dragon based in the area of the docks. When he first arrived in Cardiff, Cochfarf settled in Canton where he attended the Welsh Baptist chapel, Canton's first place of worship, established in 1853. The chapel however had seen a decline in its membership, as growing numbers of children were not having the Welsh language passed on to them by their parents. As a result, the Canton chapel became an English cause in 1901 and Cochfarf took his membership to the Tabernacl on The Hayes and stayed there for the rest of his life. In his address to the Sunday school, in April 1886, he took as his subject, *'Yr Angenrheidrwydd i Ddyfalbarhau â'r Ysgol Sul Cymraeg'* (The Necessity for Perseverance with the Welsh Sunday school). It was at the Gordon Coffee Tavern that he brought together the prominent Welshmen of the town and formed Cymdeithas Cymmrodorion Caerdydd (The Cardiff Welsh Society) in 1885, which still exists today. One of the concerns of this Welsh society was the number of Welsh-speaking prostitutes in the town. In a letter to *Seren Cymru*, the Welsh Baptist weekly newspaper, on 23 November 1906, he said that as a Justice of the Peace he regularly saw Welsh-speaking prostitutes in court. He went on to say that on his way to chapel the previous Sunday evening he heard the prostitutes on Charles Street singing the Welsh hymn, *'Iesu, Iesu 'rwyt ti'n ddigon'*.

He was elected to the town council in 1890 and made mayor in 1902. When he was appointed mayor, the Archdruid Hwfa Môn (Rowland Williams, 1823–1905) described his elevation as an elevation for the whole country: *'y mae y genedl yn cael ei ddyrchafu yn eich dyrchafiad chwi.'* He served as a councillor in a ward covering both the Welsh and Irish communities. He was an ardent Welsh Nationalist, and an Irish Home Ruler who chaired meetings of the Irish Party in Cardiff. As a stalwart teetotaller and a man of public affairs, it was a measure of the closeness of Cochfarf to the Irish community that it was he who was invited to open the Hibernian Arms in Bute Terrace, which was kept by a man named John Stack. Another one of those who bridged the gap between the Irish and the Welsh was Father John Heyde of St Peter's Church in Roath, who was a prominent member of the Welsh language society and one who had learnt the Welsh language. In 1899 Cochfarf invited 19-year-old Padraig Pearse (who would, in 1916, be one of the leaders of the Easter Rising for Irish Independence) to attend the National Eisteddfod in Cardiff, and he was admitted to Gorsedd y Beirdd (Wales' bardic order) under the name '*Yr Areithiwr*' (the orator). During his time in Cardiff, Pearse visited schools to see how the Welsh language had been introduced as a school subject.

On Edward Thomas' death in 1912, the *South Wales Daily News* said:

> Cochfarf was thoroughly alive to all the needs of Wales, and his spirit burnt brightest when in his service... he sacrificed his life on the altar of his country... Cochfarf's nationalism and patriotism had cost him dearly... but his reward was in his work.

It is a real shame that there is nothing in Cardiff to commemorate the life and work of this great man.

Robert Hughes, unlike D. Alfred Thomas and Edward Thomas, was neither a Liberal nor a Nonconformist nor a teetotaller but a Conservative Anglican who was also a brewer. He was a native of Llanegryn in Meirionnydd, and through the support of the Conservative Party he was appointed mayor for the second consecutive term so that he could be made the first Lord Mayor when Cardiff became a city in October 1905. In fact, he claimed that the Prime Minister at the time, Arthur James Balfour, designated Cardiff a city as a personal favour to him. However, due to uproar from the Liberals, he had to later apologise for making this comment. Balfour himself had real doubts about the merits of making Cardiff a city, as he told his personal secretary, J.S. Sandars, in September 1905. The same arguments are used well over a hundred years later against devolving further powers to the Senedd:

> But please remember that the only possible justification for giving the honour to Cardiff is that it must be regarded as the capital of Wales. On its merits as a British town it has no claim and, if we are to have a Lord Mayor of Cardiff except upon the Welsh ground, we should lay ourselves open to claims from every town of large population that desired to possess a Lord Mayor at the head of its Council. But if we take, as we must, the Welsh ground, do we not do something to emphasize yet further the distinction between England and Wales? And is there not, besides all this, a certain absurdity in assuming that Cardiff is to be regarded as the capital of Wales without any ground, so far as I know, based upon history, or upon general sentiment among the Welsh people?

Hughes was a prominent Anglican and the gold lectern he presented to St Mary's Church on Bute Street is still in use. His brother played rugby for Wales and Robert Hughes was at the famous rugby match in 1905 between Wales and the All Blacks when, in response to the Haka, *'Hen Wlad fy Nhadau'* (Land of my fathers) was sung for the first time before a sporting event. The correspondent, Ap Idanfryn, wrote a Welsh article on that match, much to the disgust of some Nonconformist ministers that the language was used to report such a thing, and said in language which we wouldn't use today that not only was *'hil yr hen Frythoniaid'* (the race of the Ancient Britons) represented among the 45,000 spectators but also *'y Sais hunan-hyderus, y negro croenddu a'r Jap a'r Chinead melyn-ddu'* (the confident Englishman, the black-skinned Negro and the yellow-skinned Japanese and Chinese). Many enjoyed the sporting activities Cardiff had to offer. Even Lloyd George, after visiting his first rugby match at the Arms Park in 1908, was won over: 'I have never seen it before and I may as well admit that it's more exciting than politics.'

One must not think that all of Cardiff's Welsh speakers

attended chapel. In evidence published by a Royal Commission in 1910 relating mainly to the years 1905–6, only 28.4% of Cardiff's Welsh speakers were members of Nonconformist chapels.

By the late 1870s the booming suburbs of Roath, Canton and Grangetown, with their young populations, brought a considerable influx of settlers from the West of England, and Ireland (25,000 and 4,250 respectively). This indicated a percentage of Welsh speakers not exceeding 20% if Ravenstein's assessment was adjusted downwards to take account of in-migration. From 1861 to 1871, the majority of the 21,000 migrants came from Welsh rural counties. But by the 1880s, a further 56% of the 108,500 migrants were drawn to Glamorgan from Somerset, Devon and Cornwall, plus 4% from Ireland and Scotland. The migration from outside Wales and the strength of the English language was drowning the Welsh language in Cardiff.

The 1891 census – past and present

The 1891 census included for the first time a question which set to determine the number of Welsh speakers in Wales. The aim was to see the extent of the language in each of the counties. The answer to the question would vary from either 'English', 'Both', 'Cymraeg' or 'Welsh'. It was calculated that 55% of the population of Wales were able to speak Welsh and the figure for Cardiff with its surrounding parishes had fallen to around 12%. Only 12,492 (11%) of Cardiff's population spoke Welsh, compared to 4,384 (34.47%) in the parishes. In Rumney, St Mellons, Llanedeyrn, Llandaff, Lisvane, Llanishen, Whitchurch, Radyr, Caerau, Michaelston-super-Ely, St Fagans and Pentyrch, the percentage of those able to speak Welsh was still considerably high: especially in Pentyrch (77.02%), Lisvane (64.98%), Llanedeyrn (57.35%), St Mellons (40.81%), Radyr (40.46%) and Michaelston-super-Ely (38.78%). The 1891 census data showed that the majority of the over-65s born in the town or in the parishes were recorded as being able to speak Welsh. Thus, the age-old assumption that Cardiff had always been an English town is challenged once again. In Pentyrch, Welsh remained the first language of the older generation born in the parish until the 1960s. The minutes of Pentyrch Parish Council were recorded bilingually until the early 1970s.

By 1891 the population of the town and the surrounding parishes had reached 131,261, with 40,861 (31.13%) being migrants from outside Wales and within that figure there were 29,655 from the West of England (22.59% of the total). A comparison of the 1851 and 1891 censuses shows how streets that used to be full of Welsh people, such as Bridge Street and Caroline Street, were now commercial places with many residents from other European countries. The census forms were also available in Welsh, and two who filled in their families' information in Welsh were the Rev. Charles Davies, Tabernacl, and the Rev. John Austin Jenkins, Richmond Road English Independents. In fact, both were involved in criticizing the census officials for not producing enough Welsh forms.

As would be expected in a town with nearly 30 consuls[22], languages other than Welsh or English were noted 1,100 times, and 'Irish' was also often recorded in parts of the town. Tiger Bay had developed as a multi-ethnic community from the 1840s onwards and was home to 45 nationalities. My friend, the late Neil Sinclair, who did so much to chronicle the history of Tiger Bay, said: 'part of the reason why multiculturalism worked was down to our Welsh mams and Welsh-speaking grandmothers.' The *Evening Express* in 1907 describes a lodging house which was run by a Spanish lady who 'is impossible in English but she speaks Welsh excellently'. In an article in the *South Wales Echo* in 1936, a Mrs Mahomed Ali, a Welsh Muslim convert from Grangetown, is described as 'speaking Arabic as fluently as she does her native Welsh'.

A glimpse into the past

In the 1891 census children of two years of age and under were disregarded when it came to answering the question about the ability to speak Welsh. The census covered the whole of the town, including the remaining 13 surrounding parishes that by today constitute our capital city. The survey identified 490 people who were born within the area of the study and were aged 65 years or over. The oldest individual meeting both the age and birth qualifications was one Edward John, aged 97, who was born in 1794 in Whitchurch and lived on Merthyr Road. There were three other nonagenarians: William Lloyd, aged 90, who lived in Melingriffth but was born in Cardiff town; David Evans, aged 90, of Church Road, Whitchurch, a retired tinplate roller born in Melingriffith; and Mary Williams, aged 90, of Pen-yr-Hewl Farm, Rumney. All four recorded themselves as being able to speak 'Both' languages (i.e. Welsh and English). When the youngest of the aged over-65 cohort was born in the year 1826, the population of the town was around 4,500 and that of the greater area (including Cardiff) was roughly 10,000. According to a Mrs Roberts, of the Old Sea Lock on the banks of the canal, who had settled in Cardiff in the early part of the 19th century, in an interview she gave to the *Cardiff Times* in 1905: 'when we came to live here it was like country.'

In the census, the town and the parishes were divided into four areas to determine the percentages of those over-65s and born in the area who could speak Welsh, and those who could not.

Table: Language of over-65s born in Cardiff and surrounding parishes, 1891

Area	Both	English	Total	% Welsh
Town, the Docks, Riverside, Roath, Tredegaville, Cathays	130	75	205	63
Canton, Grange, Whitchurch, Llandaff and Llandaff Yard	96	30	126	76

St Fagans, Pentyrch, Llanishen, Llanedeyrn and Lisvane	92	2	94	98
St Mellons and Rumney, Caerau, Radyr, Mich-s-Ely & Workhouse	55	10	65	85
Total	373 (76.5%)	117 (23.5%)	490	76

For clarity, 'Both' was recorded for all of the 373 people who indicated that they could speak Welsh. In fact, 75 of the 373 recorded their language as Welsh or Cymraeg. So some might have been monolingual or indicated that Welsh was their dominant language. Such a response was very common in Lisvane, Pentyrch, Llanedeyrn and Whitchurch, and no fewer than 15% of the total chose to describe their language as 'Cymraeg' or 'Welsh'. The total figure of 490 appears to be almost insignificant amongst the census of 1891 that covered roughly 130,000 people living in Cardiff town and the parishes. Yet it should erase an age-old fallacy that Cardiff had never been a Welsh-speaking town. The predominance of the bilingual sector in the over-65s born in the area, i.e. 'Both' plus those in the 'Welsh' sector, together formed a majority of 76.5%, more than three times that of the 'English-only' sector. These 490 local-born over-65s were the Sunday school scholars of the myriad of chapels that had sprung up in the town and its surrounding villages. They would have witnessed the opening of the first dock in 1839, the arrival of the Taff Vale Railway in 1841, the opening of the Rhymney Railway Line in 1858, the building of the Bute East Dock in 1859, the impact of in-migration on the Welsh language and many more of the vast changes that took place thereafter.

In 1896 the town archivist J. Hobson Mathews spoke to two Roath residents – Mary Harris, who was over 80, and Job Richards who was 70. He described Mary Harris, born in Rumney but having lived in Roath nearly all her life, as speaking Welsh much more readily than English, having known no English until she was grown up. Her daughter, aged about 50,

Ffynnon Bren, the birthplace of Job Richards

also spoke Welsh, but less fluently than English. Job Richards was born in Ffynnon Bren cottage, opposite what is now the corner of Claude Road and Albany Road, and Mathews noted 'he spoke Welsh and English with equal fluency'.

The table overleaf shows that the number of Welsh speakers varied greatly from area to area; nearly two-thirds of the population of Lisvane spoke Welsh compared with 5.6% in Grangetown. The number of Welsh speakers in newer suburbs such as Grangetown and Broadway was lower than older suburbs such as Butetown. This is shown in the *Tyst*, the Welsh Independents weekly newspaper, in 1868 in its description of the ministry of the Rev. Thomas George. It was said that he had to be an Englishman in Grangetown and a Welshman in St Mellons. In Butetown, around James Street and Loudon Square, approximately 28% of the population spoke Welsh and the farms in the parishes were still in the hands of Welsh speakers. A third of the population of the parishes spoke Welsh compared to one in ten in Cardiff Borough. The main reason for this was in-migration. The population of the parishes doubled

147

between 1831 and 1891, whilst the borough's population increased by 20 times.

Table: Percentage of Welsh speakers in Cardiff, 1891

Area	Population over 2 years old	Welsh speakers	%
Borough			
Broadway	8,569	674	7.9%
Butetown	8,315	1,249	15.0%
Canton and Riverside	25,520	2,570	10.1%
Cathays	13,649	2,042	15.0%
Gangetown	10,850	611	5.6%
Irish areas[23]	5,798	305	5.3%
Lower Splott	9,383	773	8.2%
Plasnewydd	14,468	1,492	10.3%
Town	11,406	1,528	13.4%
Upper Splott	8,258	1,248	15.1%
Total	**116,216**	**12,492**	**11%**
Surrounding parishes			
Caerau	175	42	24.0%
Llandaff	3,912	585	14.95%
Llanedeyrn	279	160	57.35%
Llanishen	692	162	23.41%
Lisvane	237	154	64.98%
Michaelston-super-Ely	49	19	38.78%
Pentyrch	1,693	1,304	77.02%
Radyr	571	231	40.46%
Rumney	516	136	26.36%
St Fagans	445	152	34.16%
St Mellons	620	253	40.81%
Whitchurch	3,531	1,186	33.59%
Total	**12,720**	**4,384**	**34.47%**
Others[24]	2,325	141	6.06%
Grand total	**131,261**	**17,017**	**12.96%**

To have a better idea of the effect of migration, I studied a sample of 1,169 (1%) of people from Cardiff Borough, split between 13 areas, with an attempt to have a balance between population and language. From the table below the people born in Wales are in the minority for every age group over 30. The large number of people under 30 is swelled by children of immigrants (72.9%). The Welsh born were also in a minority in the oldest category. The majority of the people over 60 in Cardiff in 1891 would have been immigrants from England and Ireland that came to Cardiff in their teens and twenties between 1841 and 1861.

Table: Sample of the place of birth of Cardiff residents, 1891

Age group	Total	Born in Wales	Born outside Wales
2–19	493 (41.5%)	393 (80.0%)	100 (20.0%)
20–29	235 (18.2%)	129 (55.0%)	106 (45.0%)
30–39	188 (16.2%)	82 (43.6%)	106 (56.4%)
40–49	104 (8.9%)	39 (37.5%)	65 (62.5%)
50–59	93 (8.1%)	41 (44.1%)	52 (55.9%)
60 +	56 (5.0%)	21 (37.5%)	35 (62.5%)
Total	**1,169 (100%)**	**705 (60.3%)**	**464 (39.7%)**

The lack of transfer of the Welsh language by parents to their children was also affecting the percentage. This is shown in a sample of Welsh-born residents in streets with a significant number of Welsh speakers.[25]

Table: Sample of Welsh speakers among Welsh-born residents, 1891

Age group	Total	Welsh speakers	%
2–19	1,243	184	14.8
20–29	468	171	36.5
30–39	312	145	46.5
40–49	204	104	51.0

50–59	125	78	62.4
60+	106	77	74.0
Total	**2,458**	**759**	**30.9**

The small percentage of Welsh speakers under 20 years old shows the large increase in the number of parents around the 1870s who failed to transfer the language to their children. There are several examples where the older children spoke English and Welsh and the younger siblings were monoglot English speakers. The same phenomena happened within my family in Treorchy. My father, the youngest of eight who was born in 1901 to two Welsh-speaking parents from north Pembrokeshire, could not speak Welsh, whilst his eldest brother who was born in 1882, would preach in Welsh. The four eldest children spoke Welsh fluently, whilst the younger four did not. There is no clear reason for this other than the older children who were educated through the medium of English would gradually change the language of the home. In 1886, Dan Isaac Davies said of Welsh-speaking parents in Cardiff:

> *Bu amser pan yr oedd y Saesneg yn iaith wan hyd yn oed yng Nghaerdydd. Dyletswydd rhieni Cymraeg y pryd hynny oedd siarad Saesneg â'r plant. Yn awr, y Saesneg sydd gryf, a'r Gymraeg ydyw'r un wan...*

> (There was a time when English was weak even in Cardiff. It was the duty of Welsh-speaking parents to speak English to their children. Now English is strong and the Welsh language is weak...)

Dan Isaac Davies was a strong proponent of bilingualism and he established the Society for Utilizing the Welsh Language for the Purpose of Serving a Better and More Intelligent Knowledge of English. However, bilingualism was not the common-held view of the time and many Welsh speakers (including Dan Isaac Davies himself) were failing to transfer the language to their children. Lord Aberdare, in a speech in

Cardiff in 1899, said, 'It would be interesting to know how many sons of Welsh parents in that town have anything but the slightest knowledge of such things as *"Gwlân ddu'r ddafad"*, *"bara circh"*, *"tishan froi"*, *"tishan dena"* and *"tishan lap".'* On the evidence below it seems that the answer to Lord Aberdare's question was a diminishing number. The *Evening Express* in May 1892 mentions a butcher by the name of Thomas Jones, who left an established butcher's shop in Cardiff to move to Cymmer in the Rhondda Valley to ensure that his children spoke Welsh, saying that his 'children could not be brought up to speak Welsh in Cardiff'.

From a sample of the 1891 census in Cardiff Dr Mari A. Williams, in her research on that census, shows that even when both parents spoke Welsh a significant percentage of the children would have no Welsh. In a household with only one parent speaking Welsh, the language usually was not transferred to the children.

Table: Sample showing the decline in the Welsh language from one generation to the next, 1891

Language of parents		Language of children			
Father	Mother	W	E	Mix	Total
Welsh	Welsh	112 (61.9%)	55 (30.4%)	14 (7.7%)	181 (100%)
Welsh	English	2 (2.5%)	79 (97.5%)	–	81 (100%)
English	Welsh	3 (4.5%)	61 (92.5%)	2 (3.0%)	66 (100%)
English	English	4 (0.3%)	1,488 (99.6%)	1 (0.1%)	1,493 (100%)
Total		**121 (6.7%)**	**1,683 (92.4%)**	**17 (0.9%)**	**1,821 (100%)**

CHAPTER 9

The Rebuilding of a Nation

FOLLOWING 1891, THERE was a sizeable influx of Welsh-speaking workers and their families to Splott with the establishment of the Dowlais works in East Moors. This led to the opening of three Welsh chapels in Splott: Jerusalem, Calvinistic Methodist in 1892; Bethlehem, Independents in 1895; and Ainon, Baptist in 1895. Also Welsh services were held at St Francis' Anglican Church on a Tuesday night from 1890 onwards.

However, the percentage of Welsh speakers fell again in 1901 to 7.54% and in 1911 to 6.21%, by which time every county in England and Wales was represented among the population of Cardiff. In 1901 only 3% of children between three and 14 years old could speak Welsh, around half of the figure in 1891, compared to 19% of those over the age of 65. Even the Cymmrodorion, the Welsh society in Cardiff, were affected, with a complaint made in 1903 by Thomas Owen of Cathays to Cochfarf that the only Welsh thing about them was their name:

> Will you also be so kind as to delete my name from the list of members as it seems to me that the only thing Cymreig about the society is the name – you even go so far as to print the cards with the Welsh on the back. I write this note in English to ensure it being understood.

A response to this was the establishment of *Cymdeithas Cymry Cymreig Caerdydd* (the Cardiff Welsh speakers' society) in 1904, but it did not gain the same support and prominence as the Cymmrodorion. The *Times* in 1888 said of the Cymmrodorion in Cardiff that 'the growth of the society had been phenomenal... numbering a thousand strong'. By 1909 the society claimed it had 1,250 members.

When the National Pageant of Wales, one of the most amazing and entertaining events of the early years of the 20th century, was staged in Sophia Gardens between 26 July and 7 August 1909, the intention was to celebrate the incorporation of Wales into England rather than to reinforce the awareness of a Welsh identity or support the language.

In less than a hundred years the percentage of Welsh speakers in Cardiff and its surrounding parishes had fallen from around 80% to 6.21% and the population had increased a hundredfold. On his first visit to Cardiff, historian R.T. Jenkins wrote: '... *roedd Caerdydd yn nofio ar y llanw, a'r byd (i bob golwg) wrth ei thraed*' (... Cardiff [in 1905] was swimming on the tide, and the world (it seemed) lay at its feet). It appeared that the Welsh language had been forgotten in the middle of the growth and commerce. The failure of the *Cymru Fydd* movement in 1896 must have been a blow to the patriotic Welshmen of Cardiff, as was the financial failure of the 1899 National Eisteddfod in Cardiff. It was also during this time that other Welsh chapels in the area turned to English: Soar, Independent, St Mellons, in 1900; Ainon, Baptist, Tongwynlais, in 1901; and Ararat, Baptist, Whitchurch, in 1903. From 1860 to 1903, of the 18 chapels in the surrounding parishes 15 turned to English. The stronger causes in Cardiff Borough could withstand the English domination, with only three out of 18 becoming English causes. However, in Tabernacl, The Hayes, parts of the sermon were in English; in Salem, Canton, the children's address and a monthly evening service was in English and the deacons in Minny Street felt the need to place a sign in the pulpit to remind preachers '*Iaith pwlpud yr Eglwys hon yw y Gymraeg yn unig*' (the language of the pulpit of this church is Welsh only).

This was not the end of the story of the Welsh language in Cardiff. The prediction of David Lloyd George in his St David's Day speech to the Cardiff Cymmrodorion in 1906 was correct: 'When the last truckload of coal reaches Cardiff, when the last black diamond is dug out of the earth of Glamorgan, there will be men then digging gems of pure brilliants from the inexhaustible mines of the literature and the language of Wales.' Pure rhetoric by the great orator perhaps, but in this large, bustling, multiracial city, where the English language now reigned supreme, steps were being taken that would, in time, save the Welsh language in Cardiff.

The gradual growth of Welsh nation building

With the abolition of the Court of Great Sessions in 1830, Wales seemed bereft of a national status. Strangely, it was the setting up of Welsh national teams in football in 1876 and in rugby in 1881 that let it be known that we were a nation. The Central Welsh Board of Education was established in 1896 and the Welsh Department of the Board of Education in 1907, followed by the Welsh Board of Health Act in 1919. Also, during this time, a fine civic centre was built in Cardiff, with plans for it to hold the Welsh Houses of Parliament. New offices for the Welsh Health Board built in 1938 later became the Welsh Office and home of the Welsh Government. These were early, yet important measures of devolution. The 1901 census saw the town's population grow to 164,333, with 32,000 having been born in the West Country (19.5%) whilst the total born outside Wales, 57,276, was 35% of the gross total. In 1905 the town became a city, and two years later Cardiff's Alexandra Dock was opened in 1907. Cardiff's growth continued and, by 1911, the population had reached 182,259. The West of England sent 27,473 migrants, and those from other parts of

England numbered 18,589, making an overall English total of 46,062 (25%). In addition there were 8,589 incomers from other parts of the UK, from many European countries, and from India, Africa, Arabia and the United States. By 1913 the combined coal exports from the docks of Cardiff, Barry and Penarth had reached a peak of over 26 million tons. By 1921 Cardiff's population had risen to 219,580, of which 19,398 came from the addition of the districts of Llanishen, Llandaff North, Llandaff and Ely. Those born in Wales numbered 154,531 (70.5%), whilst those born in England totalled 52,473 (24%), and those born outside England and Wales amounted to 12,576 (5.7%).

The economic slumps of the 1920s and 1930s saw a small growth of around 7,000 in Cardiff's population, despite the considerable expansion of the city's boundaries and an influx from the Valleys of many searching for work. This was the smallest increase since the decade of 1831–41 when there had been a growth of 3,890. An estimation of the city's population between 1931 and 1939 showed an even smaller increase in numbers of just 722, despite the addition of Rumney. By 1951, the absorption of a sizable portion of St Mellons led to a further increase in the city's overall numbers and, with a flurry of post-war building, the city began to expand again.

The media in Wales has played a role in increasing the use of the Welsh language in Cardiff. Interestingly, the first Welsh-language television broadcast happened on St David's Day 1953 from the Tabernacl on The Hayes. The opening words: *'Gawn ni air o weddi'* (Let us pray) were said by the Rev. Morgan Mainwaring of Pembroke Terrace (the Terrace was later named Churchill Way and the chapel was the successor of Seion Chapel). It is a shame that there is no plaque commemorating this event, but a small plaque can be found on Castle Street in Cardiff that commemorates the first radio broadcast in Wales in February 1923, with the Welsh baritone Mostyn Thomas singing *'Dafydd y Garreg Wen'* (David of the white rock).

155

As noted, in 1955 Cardiff became the capital city of Wales against competition from other towns and the criticism that it was too English to be a real capital city for Wales. The census of 1961 recorded that Cardiff's population had now reached over a quarter of a million (256,270). In 1967 the areas of Whitchurch, Rhiwbina, Radyr and a portion of Llanedeyrn were taken within the city's boundaries, bringing its population to 290,557 in 1971. The great Meredydd Evans, a well-known Welsh language activist, established *Y Dinesydd*, a Welsh-language monthly newspaper, in 1973, and other communities throughout Wales soon adopted the idea, with the *papur bro* now becoming a common sight across Wales. In 1981, despite further extensions to the city, there was an inexplicable drop in the population to 269,459.

A large majority in Cardiff rejected devolution at a referendum held on 1 March 1979. Following that disappointment, myself and other local Welsh language activists established Clwb Ifor Bach in Womanby Street in town as a place for young Welsh speakers to socialise. The club was a former British Legion Club and we had great fun taking down names of rooms such as Queen Elizabeth II jubilee room! It is a real privilege to be told by so many that they met their spouses at the club.

The census of 1991 showed an increase in the city's population to 272,557; that then rose to 292,150 by the 2001 census. In 1996 Pentyrch and Llanilltern, with a joint population of around 6,250, became the latest additions to the city's boundaries. A further referendum on devolution was held in September 1997 and, despite Cardiff voting no, the referendum was won by a small majority of 6,721 votes across Wales. This led, in 1999, to the establishment of the National Assembly in the old docklands area of Cardiff.

In March 2011 a referendum calling for the National Assembly to be granted further law-making powers was passed by a comfortable majority in Wales, including in Cardiff. The

2011 census declared Cardiff to have a population of around 350,000. Several thousand new apartments, more hotels, restaurants and student accommodation has been built within the town and the Bay area to meet the growing attraction of the capital. The opening of the Senedd, the Bay Barrage, and the Wales Millennium Centre has transformed an almost derelict dockyard into a waterfront attracting thousands of visitors throughout the year. The capital's population and that of the Valleys and Vale run like the arteries to the palm of one's hand, bringing it within the proximity of over a million people.

Further devolution has meant an increase in the powers of the National Assembly, which is now called the Senedd, the Welsh Parliament, including a measure of tax raising and, hopefully, in the next few years, the devolution of justice. All this will add to the growth of Cardiff as the capital city of a nation. These developments have helped the revival of the Welsh language in Cardiff, with Welsh-medium education being at the heart of this success story.

The quiet revival

The table below shows the ebb and flow in the number of Welsh-language speakers in Cardiff between 1891 and 2011. The numbers continued to be in the single figure percentage for every census in the 20th century. However, the last two censuses have seen a marked increase and this is set to continue in the 2021 census. This was shown in the 2018 Annual Population Survey, conducted by the Office for National Statistics, which recorded that 23.1% of the population of Cardiff spoke Welsh.

Table: Welsh-language speakers in Cardiff, 1891–2011

Year	Population	Welsh speakers	%
1891	131,261	17,017	9.6
1901	164,333	12,395	7.54
1911	182,259	11,315	6.21
1921	219,580	9,442	4.3

1931	226,937	10,862	4.79
1951	243,632	9,623	3.95
1961	256,270	11,545	4.51
1971	290,557	12,930	4.45
1981	269,459	14,245	5.29
1991	272,557	18,071	6.63
2001	292,150	32,504	11.13
2011	346,090	54,504	15.7

Welsh-language education in Cardiff

In 1893 the council undertook a language survey in Cardiff that showed that over 90% of parents were in favour of their children being taught Welsh at school. A second survey was issued stating that, if parents wanted Welsh to be taught to their children, they would have to forgo another area of education. Parents' responses showed a considerable demand, yet fewer than the first survey, but this was probably to be expected given the threat of losing an unknown school subject. Responses to this second survey showed that 8,250 (81.5%) were in favour and 1,873 (18.5%) against. As a result, teaching the Welsh language was introduced to children aged six and seven. All children were expected to learn one Welsh song and to recite the Lord's Prayer in Welsh and English every day. Welsh was made a compulsory subject in 1905 but, within two years, following another survey, this was made optional. The lack of leadership in the council in relation to the Welsh language went against the spirit of their new motto as a city: 'Y Ddraig Goch Ddyry Cychwyn' (The Red Dragon Inspires Action). Thankfully, Cardiff Council, at the time of writing, under the leadership of Huw Thomas, a Welsh speaker from Aberystwyth, is very different.

The British League of Cardiff was established in 1906 in response to the support for teaching Welsh in Cardiff's schools. The league required its members to abstain from voting for any candidate that supported the compulsory teaching of Welsh in schools. As teacher W.C. Elvet Thomas, who moved as a young boy from Fishguard to Canton in 1905, discovered, it was astonishingly difficult to maintain a Welsh identity in Cardiff:

> *Roedd rhaid ymladd pob modfedd o'r ffordd yn erbyn gelyniaeth agored a chudd, yn erbyn rhagfarn fileinig ac yn erbyn anwybodaeth a thwpdra anhygoel, ac weithiau hefyd yn erbyn rhyw ysbryd ffiaidd-nawddogol.*
>
> (Every inch of the way had to be fought for, and against hostility both explicit and implicit, against vicious prejudice and against incredible ignorance and stupidity, and sometimes against attitudes that were patronising.)

As one who was educated in Cardiff in the 1940s and early '50s, I can attest to the inadequacy of the teaching of Welsh and the general disinterest we had in learning the language. An indifferent teacher in primary school would point to an object in class and we would all recite the Welsh word. Thankfully, at Howard Gardens High School I found a far more inspiring teacher in Wynne Lloyd who did much work for the Welsh and musical life of Cardiff.

During those dark days for the Welsh language in Cardiff there were, however, glimmering hopes. In 1899 a Breton delegation visited the Sunday school in Tabernacl on The Hayes and the *Western Mail* noted how they were amazed at the teaching of the classes in Welsh. In 1905 Tabernacl established evening classes so that their Sunday school pupils could learn Welsh.

During the 1930s, in St Nicholas in the Vale of Glamorgan, David Jenkins turned his primary school into a bilingual school. In 1932 pupils from the school attended a meeting of the Cardiff branch of Plaid Genedlaethol Cymru (later Plaid Cymru). Despite coming from non-Welsh-speaking homes, those present were impressed by the standard of the children's Welsh and their enthusasism to speak the language.

Around a decade later W.C. Elvet Thomas was a successful Welsh teacher at Cathays High School. He taught Welsh to pupils who went on to make an incredible contribution to Welsh education and to Wales; three of which, Bobi Jones, Tedi Millward and Gilbert Ruddock, became university lecturers in Welsh. It was fortunate that an incident which happened to Elvet Thomas as a youngster did not turn him against the language. As a young boy of eight years old he was slapped in the face by an unknown woman whilst playing, in Welsh, with his brother outside the family home in Alexandra Road, Canton. In his autobiography he describes that moment as when he first realised *'fod gan y Gymraeg ei gelynion'* (that the Welsh language has its enemies).

In 1943, at Tŷ'r Cymry in Gordon Road, another teacher, Gwyn Daniel, and others established a Saturday Welsh-medium school. Many of those pupils at the Saturday school have made an enormous contribution to Wales, three of them being Rhodri Morgan, the second First Minister of Wales, his brother Professor Prys Morgan, and the musician Alun Guy. It is worth noting here the other contributions of Tŷ'r Cymry. The house was bequeathed in February 1936 to the Welsh speakers of Cardiff in the will of Lewis Williams, a native Welsh speaker from Llanishen. He was an early supporter of Plaid Cymru and it was said that he would greet everyone in Welsh. Tŷ'r Cymry was the first headquarters of UCAC (the Welsh teaching union), and following myself and others establishing the oldest Welsh-medium nursery in Cardiff, it soon became the home of that nursery, and it still flourishes today. The Welsh-language Evangelical Church was also established there and the Welsh Language Society has had an office there for over 40 years. At the time of writing, the future of the house is uncertain but, as its oldest trustee, I am confident that whatever happens the contribution of Tŷ'r Cymry to the Welsh language in Cardiff will resonate for years to come.

After the opening of a private Welsh-medium school in

Lewis Williams with the young Sir Idris Foster at the first Plaid Cymru summer school in 1926

Aberystwyth under the leadership of Sir Ifan ab Owen Edwards, some local authorities responded to parental demand for the provision of Welsh-medium primary schools. This included, in 1949, the opening of Ysgol Gymraeg Caerdydd (later Ysgol Bryntaf) with 19 children in Ninian Park Primary School in Grangetown, where a plaque can be found on the wall of the school to mark the occasion.

Interestingly, in a letter to Gwyn Daniel in respone to his suggesting the establishment of a Welsh-medium primary school in Cardiff in 1937, Sir Ifan ab Owen Edwards responded '... *teimlaf mai gwastraff ar amser ydyw ceisio adfer iaith i ardaloedd Seisnig Cymru heddiw...*' (I feel that it would be a waste of time to try and restore the language in Anglicised areas in Wales). He went on to note that the best that could be achieved would be *'canolbwyntio ar ddysgu darllen y Gymraeg yn yr ardaloedd cwbwl Saesneg'* (concentrate on teaching reading Welsh in the Anglicised areas). Thankfully, the visionary Gwyn Daniel and others were undeterred and his daughters were some of the first pupils in that school. His son-in-law, Michael Jones, continues Gwyn Daniel's work by being a keen advocate for Welsh-medium education in Cardiff and across Wales. The following Welsh-medium schools were opened in 1949 in 'Anglicised areas':

Name of school	Location
Ysgol Lôn Las	Swansea
Ysgol Dewi Sant	Rhyl
Ysgol Glanrafon	Mold
Ysgol Gwenffrwd	Holywell
Ysgol Morfa Rhianedd	Llandudno
Ysgol Bryntaf	Cardiff

Ysgol Bryntaf

After a few years in Ninian Park Road, Ysgol Gymraeg Caerdydd moved to Llandaff in 1954 to the present site of Ysgol Pencae.

First pupils of Ysgol Gymraeg Caerdydd[26]

162

There it gained the name Bryntaf, as the school was located on raised land near the River Taff. The policy at this time was only to allow children from a household with at least one Welsh-speaking parent. In 1966 I had to fight to ensure my eldest son could be accepted at Ysgol Bryntaf as I was not a fluent Welsh speaker at the time. Fortunately, the policy changed and this led to a huge increase in Welsh-medium education in Cardiff.

Under the leadership of Enid Jones Davies, the aunt of the folk singer Dafydd Iwan and the former Welsh Heritage Minister Alun Ffred Jones, the school grew in popularity and had to move again in 1968 to the site of the old Viriamu Jones School in Mynachdy. I'm sure this would have pleased Viriamu Jones. In 1883, at the age of only 27, he became the first principal of the University College of South Wales and Monmouthshire, before becoming the first Vice-Chancellor of the University of Wales. He was a member of the Welsh Language Board which recommended in 1900 that Welsh-speaking schoolchildren should be taught in Welsh until secondary school, and that there should be a 'systematic teaching of Welsh' in schools across Wales. However, those living in the Mynachdy area did not welcome Ysgol Bryntaf and tensions often ran high, with abuse given to pupils and staff. A blockade was also once built to stop school buses from reaching the school.

Despite the difficulties, the school continued to grow and became a three-stream school requiring a larger site. In 1975 it moved for the third time, to the old site of Cardiff High School for Girls in the Parade in Tredegarville near the city centre, currently the location of Cardiff and Vale College. By 1978/9 the school had 600 pupils and it was claimed that it was the largest primary school in Europe. This was not sustainable and, with a lack of playing fields and heating, the site was not suitable. This, in addition to continued growth, led to the opening in 1980 of Ysgol Melin Gruffydd in Whitchurch and, a year later, Ysgol y Wern in Llanishen, Ysgol Coed-y-Gof in Fairwater and

163

Ysgol Bro Eirwg in Llanrumney. A hundred children remained in the Parade under the official name of Ysgol y Rhodfa until 1983. Despite the closure of Ysgol Bryntaf, its legacy has grown year-on-year and lived up to the school motto '*Ar Daf yr iaith a dyfodd*', which means on the Taff the language grew.

Another milestone was 1962, when children from Cardiff were first able to receive Welsh-medium secondary education with the opening of Ysgol Rhydfelen near Pontypridd. This continued until 1974 when children from Cardiff, including my eldest son John, started attending the newly-opened Ysgol Llanhari near Pontyclun. This lasted until 1978, with the opening of the first Welsh-medium secondary school in Cardiff, Ysgol Gyfun Gymraeg Glantaf in Llandaff North. Again, there was fierce local opposition to the opening of a Welsh-medium secondary school at the location of Glantaff High School. My second son Hywel, on the opening day of that school, was greeted off the school bus by protesters with posters proclaiming 'Welshies go home'. Thankfully, those days are well and truly over, and things were very different when my remaining four children, Eurwen, Iestyn, Rhodri and Rhys went to Glantaf, and later some of my grandchildren, the eldest who is also called Owen John Thomas, Bethan, Rhys and Mari. Megan, Daniel and Dylan went to the second Welsh-medium secondary school, Plasmawr, whilst Teifion goes to the third Welsh-medium secondary school, Bro Edern.

Those who claim that the Welsh-speaking community in Cardiff is dependent on migration from north and west Wales ignore the quiet revolution that is happening in front of them. The increase in pupils being educated through the medium of Welsh in Cardiff – from 19 over 70 years ago, to 8,493 in 2018/19 – is a tribute to the pioneers, the teachers, the parents and the children themselves. Some of the pupils in the many Welsh schools of Cardiff today are third-generation recipients of Welsh-medium education. I foresee that the 2021 census will again show the continued revival of the Welsh language in Cardiff.

The table below shows the incredible increase in Welsh-medium education in Cardiff.

Table: Welsh-medium education in Cardiff

School	Established	Pupils in 2018/19
Primary		
Ysgol Bryntaf	1949–1981	
Ysgol Melin Gruffydd	1980	469
Ysgol Coed-y-Gof	1981	320
Ysgol y Wern	1981	623
Ysgol Bro Eirwg	1981	444
Ysgol Treganna	1987	677
Ysgol Pencae	1990	207
Ysgol Mynydd Bychan	1994	259
Ysgol Pwll Coch	1996	442
Ysgol Gwaelod-y-Garth	1968	271
Ysgol Creigiau	1977	211
Ysgol y Berllan Deg	2000	446
Ysgol Glanmorfa	2005	243
Ysgol Nant Caerau	2007	247
Ysgol Pen y pil	2007	225
Ysgol Penygroes	2009	111
Ysgol Glan Ceubal	2009	178
Ysgol Hamadryad	2016	114
Total		**5,487**
Secondary		
Ysgol Glantaf	1978	1,207
Ysgol Plasmawr	1998	1,097
Ysgol Bro Edern	2012	702
Total		**3,006**
Grand total		**8,493**

Welsh-medium places of worship in Cardiff, 2019

I have been fortunate to be a member of two Welsh chapels in Cardiff. I was a member of Bethlehem, Splott (Independent), until its closure in 1984 before joining Tabernacl (Baptist) in the centre of our capital city. These places of worship have been a beacon for the Welsh language in Cardiff and ensured a presence even during the darkest days. They are also a testament that there was a Welsh-speaking community in Cardiff long before the migration from north and west Wales from the 1960s onwards. It is a shame that an increase in the number of Welsh speakers in Cardiff has not transferred into a general increase in the attendance at our Welsh chapels. However, as this brief account has attempted to demonstrate the ebb and flow of the Welsh language in Cardiff, I am sure that the same is true of religion. Perhaps the time has come to join forces in a convenient central location, but that will be a decision for others to make. Whatever happens, I am hopeful that future generations will continue to worship through the medium of Welsh in our capital city long after my days.

Table: Welsh-medium places of worship in Cardiff, 2019

Name	Established	Current location	Denomination
Tabernacl	1813	The Hayes	Baptist
Ebeneser	1826	Whitchurch/ Windsor Place	Independent
Bethel	1827	Rhiwbeina	Wesleyan
Bethlehem	1831	Gwaelod-y-Garth	Independent
Salem	1856	Canton	Presbyterian
Crwys	1883	Richmond Road, Cathays	Presbyterian
Minny Street	1887	Cathays	Independent
Dewi Sant	1891	St Andrew's Crescent	Church of Wales
Eglwys Efengylaidd Gymraeg	1979	Harriet Street, Cathays	Evangelical
Capel y Rhath / Tabernacle	2003	Pen-y-wain Road	Evangelical

EGLWYS BETHLEHEM

EYRE STREET, CAERDYDD

ADRODDIAD

am y flwyddyn 1983

"Canys bydded ynoch y meddwl yma yr hwn oedd hefyd yng Nghrist Iesu."

Annual Report 1983, Bethlehem

Endnotes

1   I reluctantly use this term as it is well known, but the annexation of Wales is far more accurate.

2   Broadly, Senghenydd was the upland area, with Brecon as the northern boundary, Cefn Onn to the south, and the rivers Taff and Rumney to the west and east.

3   Not to be confused with the Earl of Pembrokeshire of the first creation whose title ended with his death in 1469.

4   The 1670 estimate of population is based on Hearth Tax, National Archive 179/221/294 3. Laslett, P., 'Size and Structure of Households in England over three centuries', *Population Studies*, Vol. 23, No. 2 (July 1969), pp. 199–223.

5   Leckwith was not a part of modern Cardiff. However, a large part of it was absorbed by Canton, its manorial duties and proximity to the town make it an integral part of this study.

6   Similarly, Welsh names such as Meredith, Llywelyn, Lloyd, Rhys or Rees, Gwyn, Eynon, etc. have survived without the addition of the genitive 's'.

7   From this period onwards, trade names such as Baker and Archer etc. are considered to be English surnames, except where there were three parts to the name that suggest they are Welsh, e.g. John Jones Tanner and William David Baker.

8   I've included Cae Pica as it is listed on both maps and therefore is a useful reference point. Also, it is unlikely that a farmer would have called one field by a Welsh name, Cae Pica, and the neighbouring field by an English name, The Seven Acres. This also is evidence that they have been translated into English for the tithe map.

9   The starting point for the Cowbridge carrier stagecoach was outside the Red Cow/Y Fuwch Goch.

10 The Cardiff Arms was built in 1792 in place of Y Tŷ Coch and was itself demolished in 1878.

11 The family dropped the 'ap' in favour of Williams before adopting Cromwell.

12 Pryce, W.T.R., *Language Areas and Changes c.1750–1981* (Cardiff, 1988).

13 Thomas, R.M., 'The Linguistic Geography of Carmarthenshire, Glamorganshire and Pembrokeshire from 1750 to the present time' (University of Wales unpublished thesis, 1967).

14 Not Noted.

15 The original church was abandoned after 1701. The Celtic scholar Edward Lhuyd described the church as being in ruins in 1678 after a devastating flood in 1607. The church was rebuilt in Bute Street in 1843.

16 In 1718, Alderman John Archer was charged with slandering the name of the Rev. James Harris of Llantrisant.

17 Around 1750 the cause lapsed and was re-established *c.*1770.

18 Where there is an * after the number, it signifies the number of pupils on the register where average attendance was not available.

19 Bethel Welsh Wesleyan chapel (1837), on the corner of Ebeneser and Union streets, was not mentioned in the report.

20 The trimmers' task was to ensure that the coal, as it was loaded, was distributed neatly and safely in the hold of the ship.

21 These three suburbs were not officially absorbed into Cardiff until 1874/5.

22 In a growing cosmopolitan town such as Cardiff, the number of consuls from other countries was quite

considerable: Argentina, Austria, Belgium, Brazil, Chile, Denmark, Dominican Republic, France, Germany, Greece, Haiti, Italy, Liberia, Mexico, Netherlands, Norway, Peru, Portugal, Romania, Russia, Spain, Sweden, Turkey, U.S.A., Uruguay and Venezuela. See Daniel Owen's *Cardiff Directory 1894/95*.

[23] The majority of the Irish population lived in a group of streets by Bute Terrace, called Newtown.

[24] This includes the workhouse, prison, Penylan nunnery, Flat Holm, Nazareth House, Maendy military camp, hospital, Ely Home and *Hamadryad* hospital ship.

[25] The streets were Ebenezer and Paradise Place in town, Morgan Street in Newtown, Peel Street and Loudon Square in Butetown, Cathays Terace in Cathays, and a number of small streets around Zinc Street in Splott.

[26] The first year, 1949–50. Back row, left to right: Elgar Evans, Sian Hopkin, Sian Fell, Sian Morgan, Rhys Williams, Mair Eluned Evans, Eryl Hopkin, Angharad Rhys, Sian Pierce, Teleri Jarman, Beti Wyn Jones, Rhiddian Davies. Middle row: Alwyn Evans, Derek Lloyd Jones, Iolo Walters, Ethni Daniel, Elizabeth Williams, Ifan Payne, Ceri Evans, Arfon Price, Gwyn Williams, Iwan Humphreys. Front row: Luned Rees, Iwan Guy, Mair Wyn Evans, Delyth Roberts, Gwenda Davies, Joy Llewellyn, Glyndwr Owen, Gwyn Rees, Ann George, Rhodri Jones, Olwen Rees, Ceri Payne. Absent – Ann Britton, Eryl Davies.

Bibliography

Andrews, C.B. (ed.), *The Torrington Diaries of the Honourable John Byng*, Vol. 3 (London, 1936).

Bassett, T.M., *The Welsh Baptists* (Ilston House, Swansea, 1977).

Bethany Baptist Church, Cardiff, register of births and register of deaths 1804–1837, Glamorgan Archives.

Betts, Clive, *Cardiff and the Eisteddfod* (Cardiff, 1978).

Bielski, Alison, *The Story of St Mellons* (Port Talbot, 1985).

Bishops' reports for Llandaff diocese 1771–1850, National Library of Wales.

Bowen, Ifor (ed.), *The Statutes of Wales* (London, 1908).

Bowen, Thomas, *Dinas Caerdydd a'i Methodistiaeth Calfinaidd* (Cardiff, 1927).

Brown, Roger Lee, *Irish scorn, English pride and the Welsh tongue: the history of the Welsh church in Cardiff during the nineteenth century* (Tongwynlais, 1987).

Bute Estate Letter Book, Cardiff Central Library.

Cardiff and Merthyr Guardian.

Cardiff Times.

Carter, Harold, *The Growth and Decline of Welsh Town, Wales in the eighteenth century* (Cardiff, 1976).

Censuses 1801–61, Cardiff Cental Library.

Chapell, Edgar L., *Old Whichurch: the story of a Glamorgan parish* (Cardiff, 1945).

Clark, G.T. (ed.), *Cartae et alia Munimenta qaue ad Dominium de Glamorgancia pertinent* (6 Vols, Cardiff, 1910).

Clement, Mart (ed.), *Correspondence and Minutes of the S.P.C.K. Relating to Wales 1699–1740* (Cardiff, 1952).

Corbett, J.S., *Glamorgan: papers and notes on the Lordship and its members* (Cardiff, 1925).

Daunton, Martin, *The Cardiff Coal Trimmers Union, 1888–1914* (1978).

Davies, Charles, *Canmlwyddiant Eglwys y Bedyddwyr Cymreig yn y Tabernacl, Caerdydd* (Caerdydd, 1914).

Davies, Elwyn (ed.), *Rhestr o enwau lleoedd* (Cardiff, 1958).

Davies, E.T., *Religion in Education, 1660–1775* (Cardiff, 1974).

Davies, John, *Cardiff and the Marquesses of Bute* (Cardiff, 1981).

Davies, J. Barry, 'The Mathew family of Llandaff, Radyr and Castell-y-Mynach (1975).

Denning, Roy, *William Thomas of Michaelston-super-Ely: the diary and the man* (1973).

Dowse, Leonard, *Llanishen and Lisvane: A short history of two Glamorgan parishes* (Cardiff, 1972).

Ebenezer chapel, Cardiff births and baptisms 1827–37, Glamorgan Archive.

Edwards, Hywel Teifi, *Codi'r Hen Wlad yn ei Hôl 1850–1914* (Llandysul, 1989).

Emmanuel, Hywel D., *Dissent in the counties of Glamorganshire and Monmouthshire* (1953/56).

English Wesleyan chapel, births and baptisms, 1798–1837.

Evans, C.J.O., *Monmouthshire: its history and topography* (Cardiff, 1953).

Findlay, R.J., *Ararat Baptist Church, Whitchurch, Cardiff, 1824–1974* (Cardiff, 1974).

Harper's New Monthly Magazine.

Harrison, Arthur, *Ely Methodist, A history of the church and its environment* (Barry, 1974).

Hearth Tax Assessment 1670/1, Glamorgan Archive.

Hickey, John, *Urban Catholics, Urban Catholicism in England and Wales from 1829 to the present day* (London, 1967).

Hopcyn-James, L.J., *Hopkiniaid Morgannwg* (Bangor, 1909).

Howell, John, *Cardiff 1838–40* (1884).

Hughes, H.M., *Hanes Ebenezer Caerdydd: 1826–1926* (Caerdydd, 1926).

Hughes, John, *Methodistiaeth Cymru* (Wrexham, 1856).

Hughes, J. Williams Hughes, *Troeon yr Yrfa* (Llandysul, 1978).

James, Brian Ll., *A bibliography of the history of Cardiff* (Cardiff, 1989).

James, Brian Ll., *New Trinity, the history of Cardiff's oldest Nonconformist Church* (Cardiff, 1987).

James, Brian Ll., *The Welsh language in the Vale of Glamorgan* (1972).

Jenkins, E.J., *The Splott I remember* (Cowbridge, 1983).

Jenkins, Geraint H., *Hanes Cymru yn y cyfnod modern cynnar 1530–1760* (Caerdydd, 1983).

Jenkins, Geraint H., *Y Digymar Iolo Morganwg* (Talybont, 2019).

Jenkins, J.A. & James, R.E., *The History of Nonconformity in Cardiff* (London, 1901).

Jenkins, Philip, *The Making of a Ruling Class, The Glamorgan Gentry 1640–1790* (Cambridge, 1983).

Jenkins, Philip, *The Tory Tradition in Eighteenth-Century Cardiff* (1983–4).

Jenkins, R.T., *Hanes Cymru yn y Ddeunawfed Ganrif* (Cardiff, 1928).

Jenkins, R.T., *Edrych yn ôl* (Llundain, 1968).

Jones, David, *Hanes y Bedyddwyr yn Neheubarth Cymru* (Carmarthen, 1839).

Jones, David, 'William Thomas Diaries 1762–1795', Cardiff Central Library.

Jones, David, 'Annibynniaeth yng Nghaerdydd', *Y Diwygiwr* (1863).

Jones, David Watkin, *Hanes Morgannwg* (Aberdare, 1874).

Jones, Griffith & Bevan, Bridget (eds), *Welsh Piety* (1737–76).

Jones, Ieuan Gwynedd & Williams, David, *The Religious Census of Wales 1851, A Calendar of the Returns Relating to Wales* (Cardiff, 1987).

Jones, J. Gwynfor, *Cofio yw Gobeithio. Cyfrol Dathlu Canmlwyddiant Achos Heol-y-Crwys, Caerdydd 1884–1984* (Caerdydd, 1984).

Jones, J. Gwynfor, *Y Ganrif Gyntaf, Hanes Cymmrodorion Caerdydd* (Cardiff, 1987).

Jones, J. Gwynfor, *Y Ddelwedd Gymreig Ddinesig yng Nghaerdydd c.1885–1939* (Llandysul, 2001).

Jones, John Hugh, *Hanes Wesleyaeth Cymru* (Bangor, 1911).

Jones, M.G., *The Charity School Movement in the Eighteenth Century* (Cambridge, 1938).

Jones, R. Tudur, *Glamorgan Christianity in 1905–6: A Statistical Survey* (1988).

Jones, Thomas, *The Place-Names of Cardiff* (1950).

Kennard, E.F., *Men I have known* (1918).

Keir, A.J.W. (ed.), *Roath Local History Project* (1983/4).

Lewis, Ceri, *The Literary History of Glamorgan, 1550–1770* (Cardiff, 1974).

Lewis, G.J., 'The Geography of Cultural Transition: the Welsh borderland 1750–1850', *National Library of Wales Journal* (Winter 1979).

Lewis, C. Roy, *The Irish in Cardiff in the Mid-Nineteenth Century* (1980).

Lewis, J. Parry, *The Anglicisation of Glamorgan* (1960).

Lewis, Samuel A., *A Topographical Dictionary of Wales* (London, 1833).

Little, Bryan, *The City and County of Bristol* (1967).

Llewellyn, Titus, *Hanes y Bedyddwyr yn Llysfaen, Morgannwg* (Caerdydd, 1883).

Lloyd, D.M & E.M. (eds), *A Book of Wales* (London & Glasgow, 1953).

Maps of Cardiff 1743–1841, National Library of Wales.

Mathews, J. Hobson (ed.), *Cardiff Records, materials for the history of the county Borough, from earliest times* (Cardiff, 1889–1911).

Mathews, J. Hobson, *The Place-Names of the Cardiff District* (1900/1).

Matthews, C.M., *English Surnames* (London, 1966).

Merrick, Rice, *Morganiae Archaiographia, A booke of Glamorganshire's Antiquities* (1578), ed. J.A. Corbett (London, 1887).

Merrick, Rice, *Morganiae Archaiographia, A booke of Glamorganshire's Antiquities* (1578), ed. B.Ll. James, South Wales Record Society (Cardiff 1983).

Minchinton, W.E., 'Bristol – Metropolis of the West in the Eighteenth Century', RHS' Alexander Prize (1953).

Minutes of slander cases before the Church Court of the Llandaff diocese, 1771–1850, National Library of Wales.

Minutes of the Quarter Session Courts in Glamorgan, 1758–68, National Library of Wales.

Morgan, Iorwerth, *Dechreuadau'r Ysgolion Cymraeg* (2002).

Morgan, Prys (ed.), *Glamorgan County History* (Cardiff, 1958).

Morgan, Prys, 'Hon ydy'r Afon, ond nid Hwn yw'n Dŵr: Plentyndod ar Lannau Taf' in *Merthyr a Thaf*, ed. Hywel Teifi Edwards (Llandysul, 2001).

Morgan, T.J., & Prys, *Welsh Surnames* (Cardiff, 1985).

Morgan, T., *Cofiant y Parch. Nathaniel Thomas, Caerdydd* (Llangollen, 1900).

Morgan, Thomas, 'Commonplace Book: 1708–36', in Cardiff Records, Vol. 2, ed. J. Hobson Mathews (Cardiff, 1900).

Morgan, W.T., *Schedule of Church in Wales Records, Deanery of Llandaff, Consistory of Court records, 1688–1857* (1959).

Morris, Abraham, *Hanes Capel y Methodistiaid Calfinaidd Cymraeg yn Llaneirwg*.

O'Leary, Paul, 'Anti-Irish Riots in Wales, 1826–1882' in *Llafur*, 5:4 (1991), pp. 27–36.

175

Patterson, Donald Rose, *Early Cardiff: a short account of its street-names and surrounding place-names* (1921).

Phillips, T., *Wales: the Language, Social Conditions, Moral Character and Religious Opinions of the People Considered in Relation to Education* (London, 1949).

Pierce, Gwynedd O., *The Place-names of Dinas Powys Hundred* (Cardiff, 1971).

Pugh, T.B. (ed.) *Glamorgan County History* (Cardiff, 1971).

Pryce, W.T.R., *Language Areas and Changes c.1750–1981* (Cardiff, 1988).

Pryce, W.T.R., 'Language Shift in Gwent c.1770–1981' (1989).

Pryce, W.T.R., *Wales as a Cultural Region: Patterns of Change 1750–1971* (London, 1978).

Pryce, W.T.R., *Welsh and English in Wales* (1978).

Ravenstein, E.G., *On the Celtic Languages in the British Isles: A Statistical survey* (1879).

Reaney, P.H., *The Origin of English Surnames* (London, 1967).

Record books for the census collectors for Cardiff Town 1851 and 1861, Cardiff Central Library.

Rees, J. Frederick (ed.), *The Cardiff Region, A Survey* (Cardiff, 1960).

Rees, T. & Thomas, J., *Eglwysi Annibynnol Cymru* (Liverpool, 1872).

Rees, William, *A Historical Atlas of Wales* (Cardiff, 1951).

Rees, William, *Cardiff: A History of the City* (Cardiff, 1969).

Report and minutes of evidence of the commissioners of enquiry into the state of education in Wales, 1847.

Report to the General Board of Health on a Preliminary Enquiry into the Sewerage, Drainage and Supply of Water, and the Sanitary Conditions of the Innhabitants of the Town of Cardiff (Rammell Report, 1850).

Rhaglen Eisteddfod Genedlaethol Caerdydd, 1938.

Roberts, Gomer M. (ed.), *Hanes Methodistiaid Calfinaidd Cymru*, Vol. 1 (Caernarfon, 1973).

Roberts, Gomer M., *Calvinistic Methodism in Glamorgan 1737–1773* (Cardiff, 1974).

Roberts, R.O., *Industrial Expansion in South Wales* (Swansea, 1967).

Royal Commission on the Church of England and Other Religious Bodies in Wales and Monmouthshire, 1910.

Seren Gomer.

Shepherd, Charles F., *Annals of St Fagan's with Llanillterne: an ancient Glamorgan parish* (Cardiff, 1938).

Smith, L., Toulmin (ed.), *The Itinerary in Wales of John Leland in or about the years 1536–1539* (London, 1906).

Southall, John E., *The Linguistic Plebiscite at Cardiff* (1897).

Suggett, R.F., *An Analysis and Calendar of Early-Modern Welsh Defamation Suits*, St Fagans National Museum of History.

Suggett, R.F., Awbery, Gwenllian & Jones, Ann E., 'Slander and Defamation: A New Source for Historical Dialectology' in *Cardiff Working Papers in Welsh Lingusitics*, 4 (1985), pp. 1–24.

Tapes of conversations with older residents in the surrounding parishes recorded between 1954 and 1970 by St Fagans National Museum of History.

Thomas, Brinley, 'The Migration of Labour into the Glamorganshire Coalfield 1861–1911' in *Economica*, 30 (November 1930), pp. 275–94.

Thomas, Hilary M., *The Diaries of John Bird of Cardiff, Clerk to the first Marquess of Bute, 1790–1803* (Cardiff, 1987).

Thomas, Mair Elvet, *Afiaith yng Ngwent. Hanes Cymdeithas Cymreigyddion Y Fenni 1833–1854* (Caerdydd, 1978).

Thomas, Owen John, 'Hanes y Tabernacl Caerdydd, 1813–1913', *Llawlyfr Undeb Bedyddwyr Cymru* (1993).

Thomas, Owen John, 'Caerdydd a'r iaith Gymraeg, 1550–1850' (MA thesis, 1990).

Thomas, Owen John, 'Yr Iaith Gymraeg yng Nghaerdydd', in *Iaith Carreg Fy Aelwyd*, ed. Geraint H. Jenkins (Caerdydd, 1998).

Thomas, R.J., 'Astudiaeth o Enwau Lleoedd Cwmwd Meisgyn' (MA thesis, 1933).

Thomas, R.M., 'The Lingustic Geography of Carmarthenshire, Glamorganshire and Pembrokeshire from 1750 to the present time' (University of Wales unpublished thesis, 1967).

Thomas, W.C. Elvet, *Tyfu'n Gymro* (Llandysul, 1972).

Thomas, W.C. Elvet & Lewis, Aneirin, *Ebeneser, Caerdydd 1826–1976* (Swansea, 1976).

Trounce, W.J., *Cardiff in the Fifties: The Reminiscences and historical notes of Alderman W.J. Trounce* (Cardiff, 1919).

Warner, R.A., *A Walk through Wales in August 1797* (Bath, 1801).

Welsh Wesleyan chapel Cardiff, register of births and baptisms, 1818–1837, Glamorgan Archive.

Williams, A.H., *Welsh Wesleyan Methodism 1800–1858: Its origins, growth and secessions* (Bangor, 1935).

Williams, David, *A History of Modern Wales* (London, 1950).

Williams, D. Elwyn, *A Short Enquiry into the Surnames in Glamorgan from the Thirteenth to the Eighteenth Centuries* (London, 1961).

Williams, Gareth, *Y Maes Chwarae a Chenedligrwydd yng Nghymru 1800–1914* (Llandysul, 1990).

Williams, Glanmor (ed.), *Glamorgan County History* (Cardiff, 1974).

Williams, Glanmor, *The Dissenters in Glamorgan c.1660–1760* (Cardiff, 1974).

Williams, G.J., *Iolo Morganwg* (Caerdydd, 1956).

Williams, G.J., *Traddodiad Lenyddol Morgannwg* (Caerdydd, 1948).

Williams, Mari, *Miliwn o Gymry Cymraeg* (Caerdydd, 1999).

Williams, Moelwyn I., *The Economic and Social History of Glamorgan 1660–1760* (Cardiff, 1974).

Williams, Olwen, *Lisvane Baptist Church, Brief Historical Sketch* (Cardiff, 1929).

Williams, Russell, *The History of St Mellons Baptist church, Cardiff* (Cardiff, 1906).

Williams, W. Ogwen, *The Survival of the Welsh Language after the Act of Union of England and Wales: The First Phase, 1536–1642* (1964).

Williamson, J. (ed.), *History of Congregationalism in Cardiff and District* (Cardiff, 1920).

Wilson, John R., 'The Chicago of Wales: Cardiff in the Nineteenth Century' (1996).

Winks, W.E., *History of Bethany Baptist, Cardiff* (Cardiff, 1906).

Winks, W.E., *Official guidebook for Autumn Baptist Union Assembly held in Cardiff* (Cardiff, 1890).

Wrenche, W.G., *Wrench (Pransiaid) and Radcliffe: Notes on two families of Glamorgan* (Cardiff, 1956).

Wright, Ian, *Canals in Wales* (Truro, 1977).

Young, David, *The Origin and History of Methodism in Wales and the Borders* (London, 1893).

Y Tyst.

List of place-names followed by the first date/s recorded

Town and outer boundaries Abbot's Land, on Roath Manor at Pengam (1703/3), Adamsdown (1542, 1875), Back Lane (1809) running from Angel Street alongside the castle walls, Barrah Lane (1786), Biscader's House (1729), Blackweir (1670, 1750), with Blount's Yate being displaced by the Plunge Gate with Welsh accent (1666, 1748, 1777, 1823–1837), Dobbins Pit (1491, 1492, 1550, 1674, 1715, 1778 and 1817), Dumballs (1711, 1752, 1814), Blackfriars, demolished in 19th century but with foundations marked out; Old Boring copper mills on the old quay (1777, 1788, 1794, 1847), Broad Street (1715), Heol-y-Cawl (1747, 1768, 1815), Camp Lane (1821), Gampfa (1588, 1794, 1799, 1800), Carreg Pica (1797 and 1833), Frog Lane (1821), Y Crocbren (The Gallows, 1800, 1820), The High Cross, Church Street, High Street, St Mary Street (1798), Knockers Hole (1715, 1777,1786, 1815, 1821), Mathews' Buildings, north of Newtown (1825), Nailor's shop, Smith Street (1817, 1843), the old town Bakerhouse (1833, 1871), the Old Cemetry, Adamsdown (1855, 1871), the Old Gasworks (1829, 1858), the Old Workhouse (1852), Cock's Tower (1781, 1860), Thomas Thomas Close (1610), y Gwlat (1800, 1840).

Leckwith, Rumney and others Crofft (1768), Gogofa (1725), Gwelydd-Cochion (1712), Poinmer Mary Bush (1717), Began stone (1699), Heol Costin (1726), Beili Bach (1712), Llanrhymni

(1840), Glanrhymni (1653), Coed y Cwarel (1840), Tair Erw'r
Wal (1703, 1775), Greenway fach (1731), Griffithsmoor (1702),
Pandy (1800, 1653), Castell yr Wy, Castell-y-Gwiblu (1760),
Bullcroft (1801), Bryndonlane (1835, 1809), Craig Cibwr (1653),
Gorslon (1717), Tri-Chwarter Caerdydd, Lecwyth (1764), Hewl
y Cawl (1768), Gwaun Florin Coed y Groes (1702), Tŷ Du
(1708), Tŷ Llwyd, Cefn y Wrach (1873).

Llandaff Arles (1710), Tŷ Rhys Y Gwehydd, Atlas Farm,
Baldham Bach (1670), Y Bronhau (1722), Caer-bont (1732),
Caer-Berllan (1710), Cae'r Castell (1730), Cae-Sion-Bach
(1666), Cae-y-Dintwr, Cae-y-Groes (1649), Cae-Groes-Llwyd
(1649), Cae-yr-Waun Gron (1709), Efail Ddwst (1735), Erw
Maes y Dre (1709), Erw-Pen-y Sarn (1709), Erw'r Pentre-Cae
Gwyn (1719), Erw'r Ysgolhaig (1747), Erw-Waun-y Cymdda
(1709), Erw-Wen (1721), Gwaun Syr Harri (1673), Gwelydd
Cochion Llandaf (1712), Hanner-Cnap (1713), Canton Manor
House (1852), Hanner Fach (1713), Hanner erw Llandaf (1755),
Morfa-Bach (1756), Pedair-erw Ffagan, Pen-Heol-Llewelyn-
Maerwr (1653), Nant y Gabal (1702), Pontcanna (1702), Pwll-
y-Stapse (1740), Tir-Goleu (1666), Tir-y-Coed (1747), Wedal-
Uchaf (1637), Erw'r Pentre-Cae-Gwyn (Ely, 1719), Erw'r Pond
(1719), Y Dderwen Deg (1785), Cae yr Gayll (1649), Cae-yr-
Gwyfill-y Wuan-Adam (1702), Cae'r Ofn (1702), Gwaelod-y-
Garth (1827).

Llanishen and Llanedeyrn Cae Llwyd (1653), Coed y Caeau
(1840), Craig Llanisien, Y Cwm (1683), Dau Gae y Gelli (1655),
Dolwern (1653), Lisvane Erw Wen (1721), Maes yr Eglwys
(1653), Tai tŷ Coch, Draenen Penygraig (1702, 1798), Saith
Erw Clawr y Morfa (1764) Maes y Bryn (1702), Pen-y-groes
(1765), Nant y Cymer (1702), Nant y Cabal (1702), Barwe
(1702), Cae-tir-Hywel (1702), Cefn Poeth (1702), Craig-Maes-y-
Gwynt (1702), Craig y Llwyn (1702), Ffynon-Fedw Llanedeyrn,
(1744), Erw Hywel y Goes (1702), Rhyd Lydan (1736), Tir Iarl,

Llys-faen (1653), Erw Bant, Llysfaen (1597), Maes-y-Felin, Llysfaen, Maerdy, Llysfaen (1747).

Pentyrch Cae-cefn (1761), Cae'r Yrfa (1666), Cae-yn-y-Garth (1670), Craig-Wilym (1666), Craig-y-Moel (1666), Cocket (1670, 1763), Gwaun-y-Gwayw-coch (1670), Gwern-Gladys (1670), Heol y Parc (1738), Llwyn-da-ddu (1666), Llwyn Cynfyn (1666), Llwyn-y-Brain (1666), Melin Fach (1666), Pant-y-Gwyndon (1666), Pen-y-Garn (1745), Tir-Cefn-y Gelynen (1670), Tir y Crwn (1670), Tir-Gelynog (1670), Tir-Gruffydd-Gam (1670), Tir-pen-y-Garn (1670), Tir-y-Maes Mawr (1666), Cae Ffyrling (1670), Cae Gwalchmai (1670), Craig y Moel (1666), Croes-Faen (1792), Efail y Castell, Parc-Coed-y-Marchan (1568), Pen-Rhiw-Myneich (1666).

Roath Crwys Bychan (1734), Maindy (1737), Maendy bach (1784), Hewl Plwca, Pen-y-Waun (1809), Llys-tal-y-bont (1751), Wedal Isaf (1782), Cae Budr (1721, 1803), Cae Clawdy (1814), Pont Lleucu (1705), Nant Mawr, Cyncoed, Cae'r Fid-foel (1744, 1749), Tŷ Draw (1710), Tŷ Gwyn (1809), Tŷ'n-y-Coed (1895), Celyn Bach, Coed Ffranc, Y Dyffryn, Llwyn-y-Grant Uchaf, Craig-Elin, Cefn-Coed (1702), Cymdda Bach, Cwrt-Bach, Dwy-Erw-y-Pystyl (1809), Ffynnon-Llandenis, GwaunMaelog (1653–1702), Pont-y-Celyn, Pont-Ifan-Quint, Tir-y-Tŷ Gwyn (1702), Tir Caled (1702, 1809), Tir Ceiliog (1809), Tir y Coes (1702), Hil Isaf, Hil Uchaf a'r Ysbyty (1666), Llwyn-y-Pia (1840), Y Waun Fawr (1702), Ysgybor Fach Pen-y-Waun, Griffithsmoor (1694), Gover-y-Marchog (1702), Tir-y-Spital (1777), Cae Twc (1809), Pwll Halog (1737), Y Waun Ddyfal (1801), Mynydd Bychan (1801).

St Fagans and Llys-tal-y-bont Pentrebaen (1829), Baldan-Bach (1670), Capel Llanilltern (1745), Cefn Trebaen (1666), Crofft-Castell y Gwiblu (1670), Dwy Erw y Gam Fach (1670), Erw'r Afallen (1670), Gwaun Feibion Sion (1666), Gwaun

Caled (1653), Llwyn-Crwn (1703), Pedair erw twc Llanisien (1703), Tregoches (1670), Capel Llanilltern (1745), Nant y mynydd (1653), Llwyn-y-Celyn (1653), Cabarn Plwca (1653), Cae Gwynion (1600), Cae Tir Cloi (1653), Clat Celynog (1653), Coed Cae (1673), Coed Hywel (1653), Heol Hir (1653, 1756, 1818), Cefn Coed Heol Hoiscyn (1653), Pen-yr-Heol, Maenwr Llywelyn (1653), Gwaun Galed (1653), Gwelydd Cochion Lecwyth (1699), Dwy erw Doneg (1702), Canton (1699), Cwrt Bach (1809), Y Waun Ddyfal (1803, 1835), Heol y Coed (1653), Rhyd y Lafur (1631, 1745), Heol Cefn Coed (1702).

Whitchurch Cwm Nofydd (1735, 1789), Y Deri (1735), Fforest-Isaf (1735), Heol-Goed (1653), Heol Rhiw'r Cyrph (1605, 1760), Pantbach (1731), Pant Mawr (1708), Pen-Ddywyll (1712), Philog (1811), Pwll-Wenol (1840), Rhiwbeina (1708), Rhyd-y-tywad (1731), Tir y Saith Erw (1731), Tŷ-yn-y-Parc (1810), Briwnant and Radir in the Goetre (1666).

APPENDIX B

Welsh names
for Cardiff's parishes

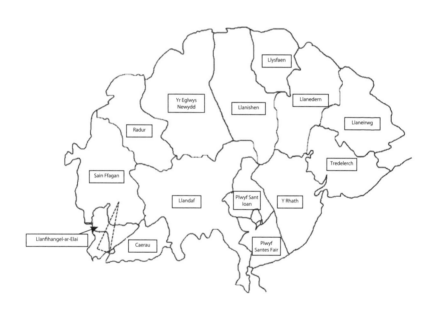

Llysfaen

Yr Eglwys Newydd

Llanishen

Llanedern

Llaneirwg

Radur

Tredelerch

Sain Ffagan

Llandaf

Plwyf Sant Ioan

Y Rhath

Llanfihangel-ar-Elai

Caerau

Plwyf Santes Fair

Welsh circulatory schools, 1738–1775

Cardiff & surrounding areas

The number of pupils on the register indicated in brackets:
St Brides, Gwynllwg 1739/40 **{36}**, Marshfield 1741/2 **{71}**, Michaelston-y-Fedw 1741/2 **{74}**, Michaelston 1745/6 **{51}**, Michaelston 1746/7 **{116}**, Bryn in Michaelston1747/48 **{60}**, Elusen-dŷ St Mellons 1750/51 **{55}**, Michaelston-y-Fedw 1750/51 **{18}**, Llusen Tŷ Rumney 1751/52 **{45}**, Llanfihangel-y-Fedw 1753/41 **{44}**, St Brides Gwynllwg 1763/64 **{77}**, Tŷ'n y Ton Michaelston 1765/66 **{59}**, Michaelston 1768/9 **{16}**, Michaelston 1769/70 **{18}**, Michaelston-y-Fedw 1774/75 **{50}**, Michaelston-y-Fedw 1774/75 **{58}**.

Llanishen 1738/9 **{56}**, Lisvane 1741/42 **{21}**, Lisvane 1742/43 **{52}**, Rydri 1753/54 **{16}**, Lisvane 1753/54 **{22}**, Tŷ dan y graig 1753/54 **{41}**, Tŷ dan y graig 1754/55 **{51}**, Llanishen Almhouse 1754/55 **{44}**, Llanishen Almshouse 1755/56 **{43}**, Llanishen 1757/8 **{45}**, Llanishen 1763/64, Graig Llanishen 1763/64 **{30}**, Night School Llanishen 1763/64 **{10}**, Rudry Church 1763/64 **{51}**, Rudry Church 1764/65 **{48}**, Derwen Deg Lisvane 1765/66 **{62}**, Caerphilly Hill Eglwysilan 1765/66 **{61}**, Tŷ'n y cae, Lisvane 1766/67 **{30}**.

St Nicholas 1738/39 **{61}**, St Andrews 1739/40 **{47}**, St Nicholas 1744/45 **{48}**, Ynys y Bowys 1744/45 **{67}**, Ynys y Bowys in

St Andrews parish 1745/46 {51}, Denys Powys in St Andrews 1746/47 {46}, St Andrews 1747/48 {40}, St Andrews 1748/49 {39}, another school in St Andrews 1748/9 {36}, Peterson-super-Ely 1753/54 {38}, St Fagans 1754/55 {14}, Michaelston-le-Pit in church 1757/58 {29}, Pen Haul, Pendoylan 1768/69 {45}, Groes-wen 1749/59 {47}, Groes-wen 1754/55 {30}, Efail isaf 1764/5 {37}, Groes-faen 1772/23 {108}, Mardy House, Radyr 1772/73 {33}, Pentyrch 1738/39 {41}, Pentyrch 1739/40 {38}, Whitchurch Parish Church 1752/53 {30}, Ffilog, Llandaff Yard 1753/54 {18}, Tongwynlais 1757/58 {44}, Tŷ'n y Cae Whitchurch 1758/59 {13}, Cwm y Fuwch Pentyrch 1761/62 {39}, Maesybryn, Llanedeyrn 1755/56 {30}, Roath 1752/53 {42}.

Acknowledgements

THE COMPLETION OF this book has been a dream of mine for many decades, one that would not have been possible without the support of my family. In particular, I would like to thank my wife, Siân, for her constant patience and support over the years, and my children and daughters-in-law for their assistance in completing this book.

I am also indebted to Dr Siân Rhiannon Williams for her valuable comments, Dafydd Huw for his help with the maps, and Alwyn Evans for the photograph of the first pupils at Ysgol Gymraeg Caerdydd.

Finally, thank you to Lefi Gruffudd, Eirian Jones and all at Y Lolfa for their support in publishing the *History of Survival*.

Author Biography

Owen John Thomas was born in Cardiff and has lived in his beloved city all his life. He learnt Welsh in his twenties and committed himself from a young age to the advancement of the Welsh language in Cardiff and the promotion of Wales as a nation. He was a strong advocate of Welsh-medium education in Cardiff and has named many of its schools based on his expert knowledge of the city's history. He was the founder of Clwb Ifor Bach and completed an MA on the Welsh language in Cardiff in 1990. He was an Assembly Member between 1999–2007 and during this time he served as the Shadow Minister for the Welsh language, culture and sport. He is married to Siân, is the father of six and a proud grandfather.